TABLE OF CONTENTS

Top 20 Test Taking Tips

1. Carefully follow all the test registration procedures

2. Know the test directions, duration, topics, question types, how many questions

3. Setup a flexible study schedule at least 3-4 weeks before test day

4. Study during the time of day you are most alert, relaxed, and stress free

5. Maximize your learning style; visual learner use visual study aids, auditory learner use auditory study aids

6. Focus on your weakest knowledge base

7. Find a study partner to review with and help clarify questions

8. Practice, practice, practice

9. Get a good night's sleep; don't try to cram the night before the test

10. Eat a well balanced meal

11. Know the exact physical location of the testing site; drive the route to the site prior to test day

12. Bring a set of ear plugs; the testing center could be noisy

13. Wear comfortable, loose fitting, layered clothing to the testing center; prepare for it to be either cold or hot during the test

14. Bring at least 2 current forms of ID to the testing center

15. Arrive to the test early; be prepared to wait and be patient

16. Eliminate the obviously wrong answer choices, then guess the first remaining choice

17. Pace yourself; don't rush, but keep working and move on if you get stuck

18. Maintain a positive attitude even if the test is going poorly

19. Keep your first answer unless you are positive it is wrong

20. Check your work, don't make a careless mistake

Arithmetic and Elementary Algebra Test

Numbers and their Classifications

Numbers are the basic building blocks of mathematics. Specific features of numbers are identified by the following terms:

Integers – The set of whole positive and negative numbers, including zero. Integers do not include fractions ($\frac{1}{3}$), decimals (0.56), or mixed numbers ($7\frac{3}{4}$).

Prime number – A whole number greater than 1 that has only two factors, itself and 1; that is, a number that can be divided evenly only by 1 and itself.

Composite number – A whole number greater than 1 that has more than two different factors; in other words, any whole number that is not a prime number. For example: The composite number 8 has the factors of 1, 2, 4, and 8.

Even number – Any integer that can be divided by 2 without leaving a remainder. For example: 2, 4, 6, 8, and so on.

Odd number – Any integer that cannot be divided evenly by 2. For example: 3, 5, 7, 9, and so on.

Decimal number – a number that uses a decimal point to show the part of the number that is less than one. Example: 1.234.

Decimal point – a symbol used to separate the ones place from the tenths place in decimals or dollars from cents in currency.

Decimal place – the position of a number to the right of the decimal point. In the decimal 0.123, the 1 is in the first place to the right of the decimal point, indicating tenths; the 2 is in the second place, indicating hundredths; and the 3 is in the third place, indicating thousandths.

The decimal, or base 10, system is a number system that uses ten different digits (0, 1, 2, 3, 4, 5, 6, 7, 8, 9). An example of a number system that uses something other than ten digits is the binary, or base 2, number system, used by computers, which uses only the numbers 0 and 1. It is thought that the decimal system originated because people had only their 10 fingers for counting.

Rational, irrational, and real numbers can be described as follows:

Rational numbers include all integers, decimals, and fractions. Any terminating or repeating decimal number is a rational number.

Irrational numbers cannot be written as fractions or decimals because the number of decimal places is infinite and there is no recurring pattern of digits within the number. For example, pi (π) begins with 3.141592 and continues without terminating or repeating, so pi is an irrational number.

Real numbers are the set of all rational and irrational numbers.

Operations

There are four basic mathematical operations:

Addition increases the value of one quantity by the value of another quantity. Example: $2 + 4 = 6$; $8 + 9 = 17$. The result is called the sum. With addition, the order does not matter. $4 + 2 = 2 + 4$.

Subtraction is the opposite operation to addition; it decreases the value of one quantity by the value of another quantity. Example: $6 - 4 = 2$; $17 - 8 = 9$. The result is called the difference. Note that with subtraction, the order does matter. $6 - 4 \neq 4 - 6$.

Multiplication can be thought of as repeated addition. One number tells how many times to add the other number to itself. Example: 3×2 (three times two) $= 2 + 2 + 2 = 6$. With multiplication, the order does not matter. $2 \times 3 = 3 \times 2$ or $3 + 3 = 2 + 2 + 2$.

Division is the opposite operation to multiplication; one number tells us how many parts to divide the other number into. Example: $20 \div 4 = 5$; if 20 is split into 4 equal parts, each part is 5. With division, the order of the numbers does matter. $20 \div 4 \neq 4 \div 20$.

An exponent is a superscript number placed next to another number at the top right. It indicates how many times the base number is to be multiplied by itself. Exponents provide a shorthand way to write what would be a longer mathematical expression. Example: $a^2 = a \times a$; $2^4 = 2 \times 2 \times 2 \times 2$. A number with an exponent of 2 is said to be "squared," while a number with an exponent of 3 is said to be "cubed." The value of a number raised to an exponent is called its power. So, 8^4 is read as "8 to the 4th power," or "8 raised to the power of 4." A negative exponent is the same as the reciprocal of a positive exponent. Example: $a^{-2} = \frac{1}{a^2}$.

Parentheses are used to designate which operations should be done first when there are multiple operations. Example: $4 - (2 + 1) = 1$; the parentheses tell us that we must add 2 and 1, and then subtract the sum from 4, rather than subtracting 2 from 4 and then adding 1 (this would give us an answer of 3).

Order of Operations is a set of rules that dictates the order in which we must perform each operation in an expression so that we will evaluate at accurately. If we have an expression that includes multiple different operations, Order of Operations tells us which operations to do first. The most common mnemonic for Order of Operations is PEMDAS, or "Please Excuse My Dear Aunt Sally." PEMDAS stands for Parentheses, Exponents, Multiplication, Division, Addition, Subtraction. It is important to understand that multiplication and division have equal precedence, as do addition and subtraction, so those pairs of operations are simply worked from left to right in order.

Example: Evaluate the expression $5 + 20 \div 4 \times (2 + 3)^2 - 6$ using the correct order of operations.

P: Perform the operations inside the parentheses, $(2 + 3) = 5$.

E: Simplify the exponents, $(5)^2 = 25$.

The equation now looks like this: $5 + 20 \div 4 \times 25 - 6$.

MD: Perform multiplication and division from left to right, $20 \div 4 = 5$; then $5 \times 25 = 125$.

The equation now looks like this: $5 + 125 - 6$.

AS: Perform addition and subtraction from left to right, $5 + 125 = 130$; then $130 - 6 = 124$.

The laws of exponents are as follows:

1)   Any number to the power of 1 is equal to itself: $a^1 = a$.

2)   The number 1 raised to any power is equal to 1: $1^n = 1$.

3)   Any number raised to the power of 0 is equal to 1: $a^0 = 1$.

4)   Add exponents to multiply powers of the same base number: $a^n \times a^m = a^{n+m}$.

5)   Subtract exponents to divide powers of the same number; that is $a^n \div a^m = a^{n-m}$.

6)   Multiply exponents to raise a power to a power: $(a^n)^m = a^{n \times m}$.

7)   If multiplied or divided numbers inside parentheses are collectively raised to a power, this is the same as each individual term being raised to that power: $(a \times b)^n = a^n \times b^n$; $(a \div b)^n = a^n \div b^n$.

Note: Exponents do not have to be integers. Fractional or decimal exponents follow all the rules above as well. Example: $5^{\frac{1}{4}} \times 5^{\frac{3}{4}} = 5^{\frac{1}{4}+\frac{3}{4}} = 5^1 = 5$.

A root, such as a square root, is another way of writing a fractional exponent. Instead of using a superscript, roots use the radical symbol ($\sqrt{}$) to indicate the operation. A radical will have a number underneath the bar, and may sometimes have a number in the upper left: $\sqrt[n]{a}$, read as "the nth root of a." The relationship between radical notation and exponent notation can be described by this equation: $\sqrt[n]{a} = a^{\frac{1}{n}}$. The two special cases of $n = 2$ and $n = 3$ are called square roots and cube roots. If there is no number to the upper left, it is understood to be a square root ($n = 2$). Nearly all of the roots you encounter will be square roots. A square root is the same as a number raised to the one-half power. When we say that a is the square root of b ($a = \sqrt{b}$), we mean that a multiplied by itself equals b: ($a \times a = b$).

A perfect square is a number that has an integer for its square root. There are 10 perfect squares from 1 to 100: 1, 4, 9, 16, 25, 36, 49, 64, 81, 100 (the squares of integers 1 through 10).

Scientific notation is a way of writing large numbers in a shorter form. The form $a \times 10^n$ is used in scientific notation, where a is greater than or equal to 1, but less than 10, and n is the number of places the decimal must move to get from the original number to a. Example: The number 230,400,000 is cumbersome to write. To write the value in scientific notation, place a decimal point between the first and second numbers, and include all digits through the last non-zero digit ($a = 2.304$). To find the appropriate power of 10, count the number of places the decimal point had to move ($n = 8$). The number is positive if the decimal moved to the left, and negative if it moved to the right. We can then write 230,400,000 as 2.304×10^8. If we look instead at the number 0.00002304, we have the same value for a, but this time the decimal moved 5 places to the right ($n = -5$). Thus, 0.00002304 can be written as 2.304×10^{-5}. Using this notation makes it simple to compare very large or very small numbers. By comparing exponents, it is easy to see that 3.28×10^4 is smaller than 1.51×10^5, because 4 is less than 5.

Factors and Multiples

Factors are numbers that are multiplied together to obtain a product. For example, in the equation $2 \times 3 = 6$, the numbers 2 and 3 are factors. A prime number has only two factors (1 and itself), but other numbers can have many factors.
A common factor is a number that divides exactly into two or more other numbers. For example, the factors of 12 are 1, 2, 3, 4, 6, and 12, while the factors of 15 are 1, 3, 5, and 15. The common factors of 12 and 15 are 1 and 3.
A prime factor is also a prime number. Therefore, the prime factors of 12 are 1, 2, and 3. For 15, the prime factors are 1, 3, and 5.

The greatest common factor (GCF) is the largest number that is a factor of two or more numbers. For example, the factors of 15 are 1, 3, 5, and 15; the factors of 35 are 1, 5, 7, and 35. Therefore, the greatest common factor of 15 and 35 is 5. The least common multiple (LCM) is the smallest number that is a multiple of two or more numbers. For example, the multiples of 3 include 3, 6, 9, 12, 15, etc.; the multiples of 5 include 5, 10, 15, 20, etc. Therefore, the least common multiple of 3 and 5 is 15.

Fractions, Percentages, and Related Concepts

A fraction is a number that is expressed as one integer written above another integer, with a dividing line between them ($\frac{x}{y}$). It represents the quotient of the two numbers "x divided by y." It can also be thought of as x out of y equal parts. The top number of a fraction is called the numerator, and it represents the number of parts under consideration. The 1 in $\frac{1}{4}$ means that 1 part out of the whole is being considered in the calculation. The bottom number of a fraction is called the denominator, and it represents the total number of equal parts. The 4 in $\frac{1}{4}$ means that the whole consists of 4 equal parts. A fraction cannot have a denominator of zero; this is referred to as "undefined."

Fractions can be manipulated, without changing the value of the fraction, by multiplying or dividing (but not adding or subtracting) both the numerator and denominator by the same number. If you divide both numbers by a common factor, you are reducing or simplifying the fraction. Two fractions that have the same value, but are expressed differently are known as equivalent fractions. For example, $\frac{2}{10}, \frac{3}{15}, \frac{4}{20}$, and $\frac{5}{25}$ are all equivalent fractions. They can also all be reduced or simplified to $\frac{1}{5}$.

When two fractions are manipulated so that they have the same denominator, this is known as finding a common denominator. The number chosen to be that common denominator should be the least common multiple of the two original denominators.

Example: $\frac{3}{4}$ and $\frac{5}{6}$; the least common multiple of 4 and 6 is 12. Manipulating to achieve the common denominator: $\frac{3}{4} = \frac{9}{12}; \frac{5}{6} = \frac{10}{12}$.

If two fractions have a common denominator, they can be added or subtracted simply by adding or subtracting the two numerators and retaining the same denominator. Example: $\frac{1}{2} + \frac{1}{4} = \frac{2}{4} + \frac{1}{4} = \frac{3}{4}$. If the two fractions do not already have the same denominator, one or both of them must be manipulated to achieve a common denominator before they can be added or subtracted.

Two fractions can be multiplied by multiplying the two numerators to find the new numerator and the two denominators to find the new denominator. Example: $\frac{1}{3} \times \frac{2}{3} = \frac{1 \times 2}{3 \times 3} = \frac{2}{9}$.

Two fractions can be divided flipping the numerator and denominator of the second fraction and then proceeding as though it were a multiplication. Example: $\frac{2}{3} \div \frac{3}{4} = \frac{2}{3} \times \frac{4}{3} = \frac{8}{9}$.

A fraction whose denominator is greater than its numerator is known as a proper fraction, while a fraction whose numerator is greater than its denominator is known as an improper fraction. Proper fractions have values less than one and improper fractions have values greater than one.

A mixed number is a number that contains both an integer and a fraction. Any improper fraction can be rewritten as a mixed number. Example: $\frac{8}{3} = \frac{6}{3} + \frac{2}{3} = 2 + \frac{2}{3} = 2\frac{2}{3}$. Similarly, any mixed number can be rewritten as an improper fraction. Example: $1\frac{3}{5} = 1 + \frac{3}{5} = \frac{5}{5} + \frac{3}{5} = \frac{8}{5}$.

Percentages can be thought of as fractions that are based on a whole of 100; that is, one whole is equal to 100%. The word percent means "per hundred." Fractions can be expressed as percents by finding equivalent fractions with a denomination of 100. Example: $\frac{7}{10} = \frac{70}{100} = 70\%$; $\frac{1}{4} = \frac{25}{100} = 25\%$.

To express a percentage as a fraction, divide the percentage number by 100 and reduce the fraction to its simplest possible terms. Example: $60\% = \frac{60}{100} = \frac{3}{5}$; $96\% = \frac{96}{100} = \frac{24}{25}$.

Converting decimals to percentages and percentages to decimals is as simple as moving the decimal point. To convert from a decimal to a percent, move the decimal point two places to the right. To convert from a percent to a decimal, move it two places to the left. Example: 0.23 = 23%; 5.34 = 534%; 0.007 = 0.7%; 700% = 7.00; 86% = 0.86; 0.15% = 0.0015.

It may be helpful to remember that the percentage number will always be larger than the equivalent decimal number.

A percentage problem can be presented three main ways: (1) Find what percentage of some number another number is. Example: What percentage of 40 is 8? (2) Find what number is some percentage of a given number. Example: What number is 20% of 40? (3) Find what number another number is a given percentage of. Example: What number is 8 20% of? The three components in all of these cases are the same: a whole (W), a part (P), and a percentage (%). These are related by the equation: $P = W \times \%$. This is the form of the equation you would use to solve problems of type (2). To solve types (1) and (3), you would use these two forms: $\% = \frac{P}{W}$ and $W = \frac{P}{\%}$.

The thing that frequently makes percentage problems difficult is that they are most often also word problems, so a large part of solving them is figuring out which quantities are what. Example: In a school cafeteria, 7 students choose pizza, 9 choose hamburgers, and 4 choose tacos. Find the percentage that chooses tacos. To find the whole, you must first add all of the parts: $7 + 9 + 4 = 20$. The percentage can then be found by dividing the part by the whole ($\% = \frac{P}{W}$): $\frac{4}{20} = \frac{20}{100} = 20\%$.

A ratio is a comparison of two quantities in a particular order. Example: If there are 14 computers in a lab, and the class has 20 students, there is a student to computer ratio of 20 to 14, commonly written as 20:14. Ratios are normally reduced to their smallest whole number representation, so 20:14 would be reduced to 10:7 by dividing both sides by 2.

A proportion is a relationship between two quantities that dictates how one changes when the other changes. A direct proportion describes a relationship in which a quantity increases by a set amount for every increase in the other quantity, or decreases by that same amount for every decrease in the other quantity. Example: Assuming a constant driving speed, the time required for a car trip increases as the distance of the trip increases. The distance to be traveled and the time required to travel are directly proportional.

Inverse proportion is a relationship in which an increase in one quantity is accompanied by a decrease in the other, or vice versa. Example: the time required for a car trip decreases as the speed increases, and increases as the speed decreases, so the time required is inversely proportional to the speed of the car.

Polynomial Algebra

Equations are made up of monomials and polynomials. A *Monomial* is a single variable or product of constants and variables, such as x, $2x$, or $\frac{2}{x}$. There will never be addition or subtraction symbols in a monomial. Like monomials have like variables, but they may have different coefficients. *Polynomials* are algebraic expressions which use addition and subtraction to combine two or more monomials. Two terms make a binomial; three terms make a trinomial; etc.. The

Degree of a Monomial is the sum of the exponents of the variables. The *Degree of a Polynomial* is the highest degree of any individual term.

To multiply two binomials, follow the *FOIL* method. FOIL stands for:

- First: Multiply the first term of each binomial
- Outer: Multiply the outer terms of each binomial
- Inner: Multiply the inner terms of each binomial
- Last: Multiply the last term of each binomial

Using FOIL, $(Ax + By)(Cx + Dy) = ACx^2 + ADxy + BCxy + BDy^2$.

To divide polynomials, begin by arranging the terms of each polynomial in order of one variable. You may arrange in ascending or descending order, but be consistent with both polynomials. To get the first term of the quotient, divide the first term of the dividend by the first term of the divisor. Multiply the first term of the quotient by the entire divisor and subtract that product from the dividend. Repeat for the second and successive terms until you either get a remainder of zero or a remainder whose degree is less than the degree of the divisor. If the quotient has a remainder, write the answer as a mixed expression in the form: $\text{quotient} + \frac{\text{remainder}}{\text{divisor}}$.

Rational Expressions are fractions with polynomials in both the numerator and the denominator; the value of the polynomial in the denominator cannot be equal to zero. To add or subtract rational expressions, first find the common denominator, then rewrite each fraction as an equivalent fraction with the common denominator. Finally, add or subtract the numerators to get the numerator of the answer, and keep the common denominator as the denominator of the answer. When multiplying rational expressions factor each polynomial and cancel like factors (a factor which appears in both the numerator and the denominator). Then, multiply all remaining factors in the numerator to get the numerator of the product, and multiply the remaining factors in the denominator to get the denominator of the product. Remember – cancel entire factors, not individual terms. To divide rational expressions, take the reciprocal of the divisor (the rational expression you are dividing by) and multiply by the dividend.

Below are patterns of some special products to remember: *perfect trinomial squares*, the *difference between two squares*, the *sum and difference of two cubes*, and *perfect cubes*.

- Perfect Trinomial Squares: $x^2 + 2xy + y^2 = (x + y)^2$ or $x^2 - 2xy + y^2 = (x - y)^2$
- Difference Between Two Squares: $x^2 - y^2 = (x + y)(x - y)$
- Sum of Two Cubes: $x^3 + y^3 = (x + y)(x^2 - xy + y^2)$
  Note: the second factor is NOT the same as a perfect trinomial square, so do not try to factor it further.
- Difference Between Two Cubes: $x^3 - y^3 = (x - y)(x^2 + xy + y^2)$
  Again, the second factor is NOT the same as a perfect trinomial square.
- Perfect Cubes: $x^3 + 3x^2y + 3xy^2 + y^3 = (x + y)^3$ and $x^3 - 3x^2y + 3xy^2 - y^3 = (x - y)^3$

In order to *factor* a polynomial, first check for a common monomial factor. When the greatest common monomial factor has been factored out, look for patterns of special products: differences of two squares, the sum or difference of two cubes for binomial factors, or perfect trinomial squares for trinomial factors. If the factor is a trinomial but not a perfect trinomial square, look for a factorable form, such as $x^2 + (a + b)x + ab = (x + a)(x + b)$ or$(ac)x^2 + (ad + bc)x + bd = (ax + b)(cx + d)$. For factors with four terms, look for groups to factor. Once you have found the factors, write the original polynomial as the product of all the factors. Make sure all of the polynomial factors are prime. Monomial factors may be prime or composite. Check your work by multiplying the factors to make sure you get the original polynomial.

Solving Quadratic Equations

The *Quadratic Formula* is used to solve quadratic equations when other methods are more difficult. To use the quadratic formula to solve a quadratic equation, begin by rewriting the equation in standard form $ax^2 + bx + c = 0$, where a, b, and c are coefficients. Once you have identified the values of the coefficients, substitute those values into the quadratic formula $= \frac{-b \pm \sqrt{b^2 - 4ac}}{2a}$. Evaluate the equation and simplify the expression. Again, check each root by substituting into the original equation. In the quadratic formula, the portion of the formula under the radical $(b^2 - 4ac)$ is called the *Discriminant*. If the discriminant is zero, there is only one root: zero. If the discriminant is positive, there are two different real roots. If the discriminant is negative, there are no real roots.

To solve a quadratic equation by *Factoring*, begin by rewriting the equation in standard form, if necessary. Factor the side with the variable then set each of the factors equal to zero and solve the resulting linear equations. Check your answers by substituting the roots you found into the original equation. If, when writing the equation in standard form, you have an equation in the form $x^2 + c = 0$ or $x^2 - c = 0$, set $x^2 = -c$ or $x^2 = c$ and take the square root of c. If $c = 0$, the only real root is zero. If c is positive, there are two real roots—the positive and negative square root values. If c is negative, there are no real roots because you cannot take the square root of a negative number.

To solve a quadratic equation by *Completing the Square*, rewrite the equation so that all terms containing the variable are on the left side of the equal sign, and all the constants are on the right side of the equal sign. Make sure the coefficient of the squared term is 1. If there is a coefficient with the squared term, divide each term on both sides of the equal side by that number. Next, work with the coefficient of the single-variable term. Square half of this coefficient, and add that value to both sides. Now you can factor the left side (the side containing the variable) as the square of a binomial. $x^2 + 2ax + a^2 = C \Rightarrow (x + a)^2 = C$, where x is the variable, and a and C

- 16 -

are constants. Take the square root of both sides and solve for the variable. Substitute the value of the variable in the original problem to check your work.

Other Important Concepts

Commonly in algebra and other upper-level fields of math you find yourself working with mathematical expressions that do not equal each other. The statement comparing such expressions with symbols such as < (less than) or > (greater than) is called an *Inequality*. An example of an inequality is $7x > 5$. To solve for x, simply divide both sides by 7 and the solution is shown to be $x > \frac{5}{7}$. Graphs of the solution set of inequalities are represented on a number line. Open circles are used to show that an expression approaches a number but is never quite equal to that number.

Conditional Inequalities are those with certain values for the variable that will make the condition true and other values for the variable where the condition will be false. *Absolute Inequalities* can have any real number as the value for the variable to make the condition true, while there is no real number value for the variable that will make the condition false. Solving inequalities is done by following the same rules as for solving equations with the exception that when multiplying or dividing by a negative number the direction of the inequality sign must be flipped or reversed. *Double Inequalities* are situations where two inequality statements apply to the same variable expression. An example of this is $-c < ax + b < c$.

A *Weighted Mean*, or weighted average, is a mean that uses "weighted" values. The formula is weighted mean $= \frac{w_1 x_1 + w_2 x_2 + w_3 x_3 \ldots + w_n x_n}{w_1 + w_2 + w_3 + \cdots + w_n}$. Weighted values, such as $w_1, w_2, w_3, \ldots w_n$ are assigned to each member of the set $x_1, x_2, x_3, \ldots x_n$. If calculating weighted mean, make sure a weight value for each member of the set is used.

A fraction that contains a fraction in the numerator, denominator, or both is called a *Complex Fraction*. These can be solved in a number of ways; with the simplest being by following the order of operations as stated earlier. For example, $\dfrac{\left(\frac{4}{7}\right)}{\left(\frac{5}{8}\right)} =$

$\dfrac{0.571}{0.625} = 0.914$. Another way to solve this problem is to multiply the fraction in the numerator by the recipricol of the fraction in the denominator. For example,

$\dfrac{\left(\frac{4}{7}\right)}{\left(\frac{5}{8}\right)} = \dfrac{4}{7} \times \dfrac{8}{5} = \dfrac{32}{35} = 0.914.$

In order to solve a *Radical Equation*, begin by isolating the radical term on one side of the equation, and move all other terms to the other side of the equation. Look at the index of the radicand. Remember, if no number is given, the index is 2, meaning square root. Raise both sides of the equation to the power equal to the index of the radical. Solve the resulting equation as you would a normal polynomial equation. When you have found the roots, you must check them in the original problem to eliminate extraneous roots.

The *Solution Set* is the set of all solutions of an equation. Many equations will only have one value in their solution set. If there were more solutions then they would also be included in the solution set. When an equation has no true solutions, this is referred to as an *Empty Set*.

Solving Systems of Equations

Systems of Equations are a set of simultaneous equations that all use the same variables. A solution to a system of equations must be true for each equation in the system. *Consistent Systems* are those with at least one solution. *Inconsistent Systems* are systems of equations that have no solution.

To solve a system of linear equations by *substitution*, start with the easier equation and solve for one of the variables. Express this variable in terms of the other variable. Substitute this expression in the other equation, and solve for the other variable. The solution should be expressed in the form (x, y). Substitute the values into both of the original equations to check your answer. Consider the following problem.

Solve the system using substitution:

$$x + 6y = 15$$
$$3x - 12y = 18$$

Solving the first equation for x:

$$x = 15 - 6y$$

Substitute this value in place of x in the second equation, and solve for y:

$$3(15 - 6y) - 12y = 18$$
$$45 - 18y - 12y = 18$$
$$30y = 27$$
$$y = \frac{27}{30} = \frac{9}{10} = 0.9$$

Plug this value for y back into the first equation to solve for x:

$$x = 15 - 6(0.9) = 15 - 5.4 = 9.6$$

Check both equations if you have time:

$$9.6 + 6(0.9) = 9.6 + 5.4 = 15$$

$$3(9.6) - 12(0.9) = 28.8 - 10.8 = 18$$

Therefore, the solution is $(9.6, 0.9)$.

To solve a system of equations using *elimination*, begin by rewriting both equations in standard form $Ax + By = C$. Check to see if the coefficients of one pair of like variables add to zero. If not, multiply one or both of the equations by a non-zero number to make one set of like variables add to zero. Add the two equations to solve for one of the variables. Substitute this value into one of the original equations to solve for the other variable. Check your work by substituting into the other equation. Next we will solve the same problem as above, but using the addition method.

Solve the system using elimination:

$$x + 6y = 15$$

$$3x - 12y = 18$$

If we multiply the first equation by 2, we can eliminate the y terms:

$$2x + 12y = 30$$

$$3x - 12y = 18$$

Add the equations together and solve for x:

$$5x = 48$$

$$x = \frac{48}{5} = 9.6$$

Plug the value for x back in to either of the original equations and solve for y:

$$9.6 + 6y = 15$$

$$y = \frac{15 - 9.6}{6} = 0.9$$

Check both equations if you have time:

$9.6 + 6(0.9) = 9.6 + 5.4 = 15$

$3(9.6) - 12(0.9) = 28.8 - 10.8 = 18$

Therefore, the solution is $(9.6, 0.9)$.

Equations and Graphing

When algebraic functions and equations are shown graphically, they are usually shown on a *Cartesian Coordinate Plane*. The Cartesian coordinate plane consists of two number lines placed perpendicular to each other, and intersecting at the zero point, also known as the origin. The horizontal number line is known as the x-axis, with positive values to the right of the origin, and negative values to the left of the origin. The vertical number line is known as the y-axis, with positive values above the origin, and negative values below the origin. Any point on the plane can be identified by an ordered pair in the form (x, y), called coordinates. The x-value of the coordinate is called the abscissa, and the y-value of the coordinate is called the ordinate. The two number lines divide the plane into four quadrants: I, II, III, and IV.

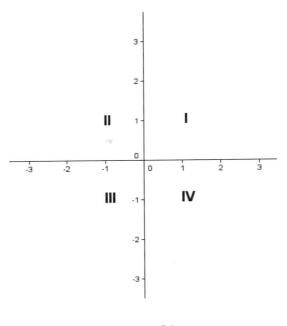

Before learning the different forms equations can be written in, it is important to understand some terminology. A ratio of the change in the vertical distance to the change in horizontal distance is called the *Slope*. On a graph with two points, (x_1, y_1) and (x_2, y_2), the slope is represented by the formula $= \frac{y_2 - y_1}{x_2 - x_1}$; $x_1 \neq x_2$. If the value of the slope is positive, the line slopes upward from left to right. If the value of the slope is negative, the line slopes downward from left to right. If the y-coordinates are the same for both points, the slope is 0 and the line is a *Horizontal Line*. If the x-coordinates are the same for both points, there is no slope and the line is a *Vertical Line*. Two or more lines that have equal slopes are *Parallel Lines*. *Perpendicular Lines* have slopes that are negative reciprocals of each other, such as $\frac{a}{b}$ and $\frac{-b}{a}$.

As mentioned previously, equations can be written many ways. Below is a list of the many forms equations can take.

- *Standard Form*: $Ax + By = C$; the slope is $\frac{-A}{B}$ and the y-intercept is $\frac{C}{B}$
- *Slope Intercept Form*: $y = mx + b$, where m is the slope and b is the y-intercept
- *Point-Slope Form*: $y - y_1 = m(x - x_1)$, where m is the slope and (x_1, y_1) is a point on the line
- *Two-Point Form*: $\frac{y - y_1}{x - x_1} = \frac{y_2 - y_1}{x_2 - x_1}$, where (x_1, y_1) and (x_2, y_2) are two points on the given line
- *Intercept Form*: $\frac{x}{x_1} + \frac{y}{y_1} = 1$, where $(x_1, 0)$ is the point at which a line intersects the x-axis, and $(0, y_1)$ is the point at which the same line intersects the y-axis

Equations can also be written as $ax + b = 0$, where $a \neq 0$. These are referred to as *One Variable Linear Equations*. A solution to such an equation is called a *Root*. In the case where we have the equation $5x + 10 = 0$, if we solve for x we get a solution of $x = -2$. In other words, the root of the equation is -2. This is found by first subtracting 10 from both sides, which gives $5x = -10$. Next, simply divide both sides by the coefficient of the variable, in this case 5, to get $x = -2$. This can be checked by plugging -2 back into the original equation $(5)(-2) + 10 = -10 + 10 = 0$.

Calculations Using Points

Sometimes you need to perform calculations using only points on a graph as input data. Using points, you can determine what the midpoint and distance are. If you know the equation for a line you can calculate the distance between the line and the point.

To find the *Midpoint* of two points (x_1, y_1) and (x_2, y_2), average the x-coordinates to get the x-coordinate of the midpoint, and average the y-coordinates to get the y-coordinate of the midpoint. The formula is midpoint $= \left(\frac{x_1+x_2}{2}, \frac{y_1+y_2}{2}\right)$.

The *Distance* between two points is the same as the length of the hypotenuse of a right triangle with the two given points as endpoints, and the two sides of the right triangle parallel to the x-axis and y-axis, respectively. The length of the segment parallel to the x-axis is the difference between the x-coordinates of the two points. The length of the segment parallel to the y-axis is the difference between the y-coordinates of the two points. Use the Pythagorean Theorem $a^2 + b^2 = c^2$ or $c = \sqrt{a^2 + b^2}$ to find the distance. The formula is:
distance $= \sqrt{(x_2 - x_1)^2 + (y_2 - y_1)^2}$.

When a line is in the format $Ax + By + C = 0$, where A, B, and C are coefficients, you can use a point (x_1, y_1) not on the line and apply the formula $d = \frac{|Ax_1 + By_1 + C|}{\sqrt{A^2 + B^2}}$ to find the distance between the line and the point (x_1, y_1).

Functions

A function is an equation that has exactly one value of output variable (dependent variable) for each value of the input variable (independent variable). The set of all values for the input variable (here assumed to be x) is the domain of the function, and the set of all corresponding values of output variable (here assumed to be y) is the range of the function. When looking at a graph of an equation, the easiest way to determine if the equation is a function or not is to conduct the vertical line test. If a vertical line drawn through any value of x crosses the graph in more than one place, the equation is not a function.

In functions with the notation $f(x)$, the value substituted for x in the equation is called the argument. The domain is the set of all values for x in a function. Unless otherwise given, assume the domain is the set of real numbers that will yield real numbers for the range. This is the domain of definition.

The graph of a function is the set of all ordered pairs (x, y) that satisfy the equation of the function. The points that have zero as the value for y are called the zeros of the function. These are also the x-intercepts, because that is the point at which the graph crosses, or intercepts, the x-axis. The points that have zero as the value for x are the y-intercepts because that is where the graph crosses the y-axis.

Any time there are vertical asymptotes or holes in a graph, such that the complete graph cannot be drawn as one continuous line, a graph is said to have discontinuities. Examples would include the graphs of hyperbolas that are functions, and the function $f(x) = \tan x$.

Manipulation of Functions

Horizontal and vertical shift occur when values are added to or subtracted from the x or y values, respectively.

If a constant is added to the y portion of each point, the graph shifts up. If a constant is subtracted from the y portion of each point, the graph shifts down. This is represented by the expression $f(x) \pm k$, where k is a constant.

If a constant is added to the x portion of each point, the graph shifts left. If a constant is subtracted from the x portion of each point, the graph shifts right. This is represented by the expression $f(x \pm k)$, where k is a constant.

Stretch, compression, and reflection occur when different parts of a function are multiplied by different groups of constants. If the function as a whole is multiplied by a real number constant greater than 1 ($k \times f(x)$), the graph is stretched vertically. If k in the previous equation is greater than zero but less than 1, the graph is compressed vertically. If k is less than zero, the graph is reflected about the x-axis, in addition to being either stretched or compressed vertically if k is less than or greater than -1, respectively.

If instead, just the x-term is multiplied by a constant greater than 1 ($f(k \times x)$), the graph is compressed horizontally. If k in the previous equation is greater than zero but less than 1, the graph is stretched horizontally. If k is less than zero, the graph is reflected about the y-axis, in addition to being either stretched or compressed horizontally if k is greater than or less than -1, respectively.

Classification of Functions

There are many different ways to classify functions based on their structure or behavior. Listed here are a few common classifications.

Constant functions are given by the equation $y = $ b or $f(x) = b$, where b is a real number. There is no independent variable present in the equation, so the function has a constant value for all x. The graph of a constant function is a horizontal line of slope 0 that is positioned b units from the x-axis. If b is positive, the line is above the x-axis; if b is negative, the line is below the x-axis.

Identity functions are identified by the equation $y = x$ or $f(x) = x$, where every value of y is equal to its corresponding value of x. The only zero is the point $(0, 0)$. The graph is a diagonal line with slope 1.

In **linear functions**, the value of the function changes in direct proportion to x. The rate of change, represented by the slope on its graph, is constant throughout. The standard form of a linear equation is $ax + by = c$, where a, b, and c are real numbers. As a function, this equation is commonly written as $y = mx + b$ or $f(x) = mx + b$. This is known as the slope-intercept form, because the coefficients give the slope of the graphed function (m) and its y-intercept (b). Solve the equation $mx + b = 0$ for x to get $x = -\frac{b}{m}$, which is the only zero of the function. The domain and range are both the set of all real numbers.

A **polynomial function** is a function with multiple terms and multiple powers of x, such as

$$f(x) = a_n x^n + a_{n-1} x^{n-1} + a_{n-2} x^{n-2} + \cdots + a_1 x + a_0$$

where n is a non-negative integer that is the highest exponent in the polynomial, and $a_n \neq 0$. The domain of a polynomial function is the set of all real numbers. If the greatest exponent in the polynomial is even, the polynomial is said to be of even degree and the range is the set of real numbers that satisfy the function. If the greatest exponent in the polynomial is odd, the polynomial is said to be odd and the range, like the domain, is the set of all real numbers.

A **quadratic function** is a polynomial function that follows the equation pattern $y = ax^2 + bx + c$, or $f(x) = ax^2 + bx + c$, where a, b, and c are real numbers and $a \neq 0$. The domain of a quadratic function is the set of all real numbers. The range is also real numbers, but only those in the subset of the domain that satisfy the equation. To determine the number of roots of a quadratic equation, solve the expression $b^2 - 4ac$. If this value is positive, there are two unique real roots. If this value equals zero, there is one real root, which is a double root. If this value is less than zero, there are no real roots. The root(s) of any quadratic function can be found by plugging the values of a, b, and c into the **quadratic formula**:

$$x = \frac{-b \pm \sqrt{b^2 - 4ac}}{2a}$$

If the expression $b^2 - 4ac$ is negative, you will instead find complex roots. A quadratic function has a parabola for its graph. In the equation $f(x) = ax^2 + bx + c$, if a is positive, the parabola will open upward. If a is negative, the parabola will open downward. The axis of symmetry is a vertical line that passes through the vertex. To determine whether or not the parabola will intersect the x-axis, check the number of real roots. An equation with two real roots will cross the x-axis twice. An equation with one real root will have its vertex on the x-axis. An equation with no real roots will not contact the x-axis.

A **rational function** is a function that can be constructed as a ratio of two polynomial expressions: $f(x) = \frac{p(x)}{q(x)}$, where $p(x)$ and $q(x)$ are both polynomial expressions and $q(x) \neq 0$. The domain is the set of all real numbers, except any values for which $q(x) = 0$. The range is the set of real numbers that satisfies the function when the domain is applied. When you graph a rational function, you will have vertical asymptotes wherever $q(x) = 0$. If the polynomial in the numerator is of lesser degree than the polynomial in the denominator, the x-axis will also be a horizontal asymptote. If the numerator and denominator have equal degrees, there will be a horizontal asymptote not on the x-axis. If the degree of the numerator is exactly one greater than the degree of the denominator, the graph will have an oblique, or diagonal, asymptote. The asymptote will be along the line $y = \frac{p_n}{q_{n-1}} x + \frac{p_{n-1}}{q_{n-1}}$, where p_n and q_{n-1} are the coefficients of the highest degree terms in their respective polynomials.

A **square root function** is a function that contains a radical and is in the format $f(x) = \sqrt{ax + b}$. The domain is the set of all real numbers that yields a positive radicand or a radicand equal to zero. Because square root values are assumed to be

- 27 -

positive unless otherwise identified, the range is all real numbers from zero to infinity. To find the zero of a square root function, set the radicand equal to zero and solve for *x*. The graph of a square root function is always to the right of the zero and always above the *x*-axis.

An **absolute value function** is in the format $f(x) = |ax + b|$. Like other functions, the domain is the set of all real numbers. However, because absolute value indicates positive numbers, the range is limited to positive real numbers. To find the zero of an absolute value function, set the portion inside the absolute value sign equal to zero and solve for x. An absolute value function is also known as a piecewise function because it must be solved in pieces – one for if the value inside the absolute value sign is positive, and one for if the value is negative. The function can be expressed as

$$f(x) = \begin{cases} ax + b & \text{if } ax + b \geq 0 \\ -(ax + b) & \text{if } ax + b < 0 \end{cases}$$

This will allow for an accurate statement of the range.

Exponential functions are equations that have the format $y = b^x$, where base $b > 0$ and
$b \neq 1$. The exponential function can also be written $f(x) = b^x$. **Logarithmic functions** are equations that have the format $y = \log_b x$ or $f(x) = \log_b x$. The base b may be any number except one; however, the most common bases for logarithms are base 10 and base e. The log base e is known the natural logarithm, or *ln*, expressed by the function $f(x) = \ln x$. Any logarithm that does not have an assigned value of b is assumed to be base 10: $\log x = \log_{10} x$. Exponential functions and logarithmic functions are related in that one is the inverse of the other. If $f(x) = b^x$, then $f^{-1}(x) = \log_b x$. This can perhaps be expressed more clearly by the two equations: $y = b^x$ and $x = \log_b y$.

The following properties apply to logarithmic expressions:

$$\log_b 1 = 0$$

$$\log_b b = 1$$

$$\log_b b^p = p$$

$$\log_b MN = \log_b M + \log_b N$$

$$\log_b \frac{M}{N} = \log_b M - \log_b N$$

$$\log_b M^p = p \log_b M$$

In a **one-to-one function**, each value of x has exactly one value for y (this is the definition of a function) *and* each value of y has exactly one value for x. While the vertical line test will determine if a graph is that of a function, the horizontal line test will determine if a function is a one-to-one function. If a horizontal line drawn at any value of y intersects the graph in more than one place, the graph is not that of a one-to-one function. Do not make the mistake of using the horizontal line test exclusively in determining if a graph is that of a one-to-one function. A one-to-one function must pass both the vertical line test and the horizontal line test. One-to-one functions are also **invertible functions**.

A **monotone function** is a function whose graph either constantly increases or constantly decreases. Examples include the functions $f(x) = x$, $f(x) = -x$, or $f(x) = x^3$.

An **even function** has a graph that is symmetric with respect to the y-axis and satisfies the equation $f(x) = f(-x)$. Examples include the functions $f(x) = x^2$ and $f(x) = ax^n$, where a is any real number and n is a positive even integer.

An **odd function** has a graph that is symmetric with respect to the origin and satisfies the equation $f(x) = -f(-x)$. Examples include the functions $f(x) = x^3$ and $f(x) = ax^n$, where a is any real number and n is a positive odd integer.

Algebraic functions are those that exclusively use polynomials and roots. These would include polynomial functions, rational functions, square root functions, and all combinations of these functions, such as polynomials as the radicand. These combinations may be joined by addition, subtraction, multiplication, or division, but may not include variables as exponents.

Transcendental functions are all functions that are non-algebraic. Any function that includes logarithms, trigonometric functions, variables as exponents, or any combination that includes any of these is not algebraic in nature, even if the function includes polynomials or roots.

Related concepts

According to the **Fundamental Theorem of Algebra**, every non-constant, single variable polynomial has exactly as many roots as the polynomial's highest exponent. For example, if x^4 is the largest exponent of a term, the polynomial will have exactly 4 roots. However, some of these roots may have multiplicity or be non-real numbers. For instance, in the polynomial function $f(x) = x^4 - 4x + 3$, the only real roots are 1 and -1. The root 1 has multiplicity of 2 and there is one non-real root $(-1 - \sqrt{2}i)$.

The **Remainder Theorem** is useful for determining the remainder when a polynomial is divided by a binomial. The Remainder Theorem states that if a polynomial function $f(x)$ is divided by a binomial $x - a$, where a is a real number, the remainder of the division will be the value of $f(a)$. If $f(a) = 0$, then a is a root of the polynomial.

The **Factor Theorem** is related to the Remainder Theorem and states that if $f(a) = 0$ then $(x - a)$ is a factor of the function.

According to the **Rational Root Theorem,** any rational root of a polynomial function
$f(x) = a_n x^n + a_{n-1} x^{n-1} + \cdots + a_1 x + a_0$ with integer coefficients will, when reduced to its lowest terms, be a positive or negative fraction such that the numerator is a factor of a_0 and the denominator is a factor of a_n. For instance, if the polynomial function $f(x) = x^3 + 3x^2 - 4$ has any rational roots, the numerators of

those roots can only be factors of 4 (1, 2, 4), and the denominators can only be

factors of 1 (1). The function in this example has roots of 1 (or $\frac{1}{1}$) and -2 (or $-\frac{2}{1}$).

Variables that vary directly are those that either both increase at the same rate or both decrease at the same rate. For example, in the functions $f(x) = kx$ or $f(x) = kx^n$, where k and n are positive, the value of $f(x)$ increases as the value of x increases and decreases as the value of x decreases.

Variables that vary inversely are those where one increases while the other decreases. For example, in the functions $f(x) = \frac{k}{x}$ or $f(x) = \frac{k}{x^n}$ where k is a positive constant, the value of y increases as the value of x decreases, and the value of y decreases as the value of x increases.

In both cases, k is constant of variation.

Applying the Basic Operations to Functions

For each of the basic functions, we will use these functions as examples: $f(x) = x^2$ and $g(x) = x$.

To find the sum of two functions f and g, assuming the domains are compatible, simply add the two functions together: $(f + g)(x) = f(x) + g(x) = x^2 + x$

To find the difference of two functions f and g, assuming the domains are compatible, simply subtract the second function from the first: $(f - g)(x) = f(x) - g(x) = x^2 - x$.

To find the product of two functions f and g, assuming the domains are compatible, multiply the two functions together: $(f \cdot g)(x) = f(x) \cdot g(x) = x^2 \cdot x = x^3$.

To find the quotient of two functions f and g, assuming the domains are compatible, divide the first function by the second: $\frac{f}{g}(x) = \frac{f(x)}{g(x)} = \frac{x^2}{x} = x \; ; x \neq 0$.

The example given in each case is fairly simple, but on a given problem, if you are looking only for the value of the sum, difference, product or quotient of two functions at a particular x-value, it may be simpler to solve the functions individually and then perform the given operation using those values.

- 31 -

The composite of two functions f and g, written as $(f \circ g)(x)$ simply means that the output of the second function is used as the input of the first. This can also be written as $f(g(x))$. In general, this can be solved by substituting $g(x)$ for all instances of x in $f(x)$ and simplifying. Using the example functions $f(x) = x^2 - x + 2$ and $g(x) = x + 1$, we can find that $(f \circ g)(x)$ or $f(g(x))$ is equal to $f(x + 1) = (x + 1)^2 - (x + 1) + 2$, which simplifies to $x^2 + x + 2$.

It is important to note that $(f \circ g)(x)$ is not necessarily the same as $(g \circ f)(x)$. The process is not commutative like addition or multiplication expressions. If $(f \circ g)(x)$ does equal $(g \circ f)(x)$, the two functions are inverses of each other.

Trigonometry

The three basic trigonometric functions are sine, cosine, and tangent.

Sine

The sine (sin) function has a period of $360°$ or 2π radians. This means that its graph makes one complete cycle every $360°$ or 2π. Because $\sin 0 = 0$, the graph of $y = \sin x$ begins at the origin, with the x-axis representing the angle measure, and the y-axis representing the sine of the angle. The graph of the sine function is a smooth curve that begins at the origin, peaks at the point $\left(\frac{\pi}{2}, 1\right)$, crosses the x-axis at $(\pi, 0)$, has its lowest point at $\left(\frac{3\pi}{2}, -1\right)$, and returns to the x-axis to complete one cycle at $(2\pi, 0)$.

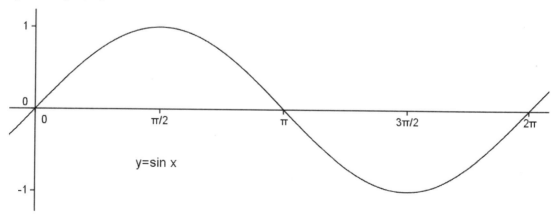

Cosine

The cosine (cos) function also has a period of 360° or 2π radians, which means that its graph also makes one complete cycle every 360° or 2π. Because cos 0° = 1, the graph of $y = \cos x$ begins at the point $(0, 1)$, with the x-axis representing the angle measure, and the y-axis representing the cosine of the angle. The graph of the cosine function is a smooth curve that begins at the point $(0, 1)$, crosses the x-axis at the point $\left(\frac{\pi}{2}, 0\right)$, has its lowest point at $(\pi, -1)$, crosses the x-axis again at the point $\left(\frac{3\pi}{2}, 0\right)$, and returns to a peak at the point $(2\pi, 1)$ to complete one cycle.

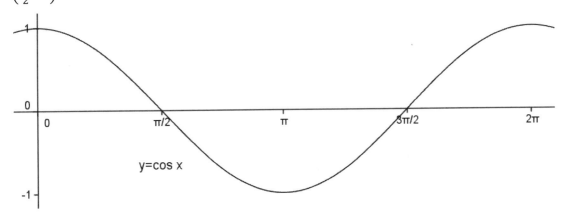

Tangent

The tangent (tan) function has a period of 180° or π radians, which means that its graph makes one complete cycle every 180° or π radians. The x-axis represents the angle measure, and the y-axis represents the tangent of the angle. The graph of the tangent function is a series of smooth curves that cross the x-axis at every 180° or π radians and have an asymptote every $k \cdot 90°$ or $\frac{k\pi}{2}$ radians, where k is an odd integer. This can be explained by the fact that the tangent is calculated by dividing the sine by the cosine, since the cosine equals zero at those asymptote points.

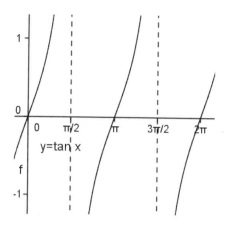

Defined and Reciprocal Functions

The tangent function is defined as the ratio of the sine to the cosine:

Tangent (tan):

$$\tan x = \frac{\sin x}{\cos x}$$

To take the reciprocal of a number means to place that number as the denominator of a fraction with a numerator of 1. The reciprocal functions are thus defined quite simply.

Cosecant (csc):

$$\csc x = \frac{1}{\sin x}$$

Secant (sec):

$$\sec x = \frac{1}{\cos x}$$

Cotangent (cot):

$$\cot x = \frac{1}{\tan x}$$

It is important to know these reciprocal functions, but they are not as commonly used as the three basic functions.

Inverse Functions

Each of the trigonometric functions accepts an angular measure, either degrees or radians, and gives a numerical value as the output. The inverse functions do the opposite; they accept a numerical value and give an angular measure as the output. The inverse sine, or arcsine, commonly written as either $\sin^{-1} x$ or $\arcsin x$, gives the angle whose sine is x. Similarly:

The inverse of $\cos x$ is written as $\cos^{-1} x$ or $\arccos x$ and means the angle whose cosine is x.

The inverse of $\tan x$ is written as $\tan^{-1} x$ or $\arctan x$ and means the angle whose tangent is x.

The inverse of $\csc x$ is written as $\csc^{-1} x$ or $\operatorname{arccsc} x$ and means the angle whose cosecant is x.

The inverse of $\sec x$ is written as $\sec^{-1} x$ or $\operatorname{arcsec} x$ and means the angle whose secant is x.

The inverse of $\cot x$ is written as $\cot^{-1} x$ or $\operatorname{arccot} x$ and means the angle whose cotangent is x.

Important note about solving trigonometric equations

Trigonometric and algebraic equations are solved following the same rules, but while algebraic expressions have one unique solution, trigonometric equations could have multiple solutions, and you must find them all. When solving for an angle with a known trigonometric value, you must consider the sign and include all angles with that value. Your calculator will probably only give one value as an answer, typically in the following ranges:

For the inverse sine function, $\left[-\frac{\pi}{2}, \frac{\pi}{2}\right]$ or $[-90°, 90°]$

For the inverse cosine function, $[0, \pi]$ or $[0°, 180°]$

For the inverse tangent function, $\left[-\frac{\pi}{2}, \frac{\pi}{2}\right]$ or $[-90°, 90°]$

It is important to determine if there is another angle in a different quadrant that also satisfies the problem. To do this, find the other quadrant(s) with the same sign for that trigonometric function and find the angle that has the same reference angle. Then check whether this angle is also a solution.

In the first quadrant, all six trigonometric functions are positive (sin, cos, tan, csc, sec, cot).

In the second quadrant, sin and csc are positive.

In the third quadrant, tan and cot are positive.

In the fourth quadrant, cos and sec are positive.

If you remember the phrase, "ALL Students Take Classes," you will be able to remember the sign of each trigonometric function in each quadrant. ALL represents all the signs in the first quadrant. The "S" in "Students" represents the sine function and its reciprocal in the second quadrant. The "T" in "Take" represents the tangent function and its reciprocal in the third quadrant. The "C" in "Classes" represents the cosine function and its reciprocal.

Trigonometric Identities

<u>Sum and Difference</u>

To find the sine, cosine, or tangent of the sum or difference of two angles, use one of the following formulas:

$$\sin(\alpha \pm \beta) = \sin \alpha \cos \beta \pm \cos \alpha \sin \beta$$
$$\cos(\alpha \pm \beta) = \cos \alpha \cos \beta \mp \sin \alpha \sin \beta$$
$$\tan(\alpha \pm \beta) = \frac{\tan \alpha \pm \tan \beta}{1 \mp \tan \alpha \tan \beta}$$

where α and β are two angles with known sine, cosine, or tangent values as needed.

<u>Half angle</u>

To find the sine or cosine of half of a known angle, use the following formulas:

$$\sin\frac{\theta}{2} = \pm\sqrt{\frac{1-\cos\theta}{2}}$$

$$\cos\frac{\theta}{2} = \pm\sqrt{\frac{1+\cos\theta}{2}}$$

where θ is an angle with a known exact cosine value.

To determine the sign of the answer, you must notice the quadrant the given angle is in and apply the correct sign for the trigonometric function you are using. If you need to find the exact sine or cosine of an angle that you do not know, such as sin 22.5°, you can rewrite the given angle as a half angle, such as $\sin\frac{45°}{2}$, and use the formula above.

To find the tangent or cotangent of half of a known angle, use the following formulas:

$$\tan\frac{\theta}{2} = \frac{\sin\theta}{1+\cos\theta}$$

$$\cot\frac{\theta}{2} = \frac{\sin\theta}{1-\cos\theta}$$

where θ is an angle with known exact sine and cosine values.

These formulas will work for finding the tangent or cotangent of half of any angle unless the cosine of θ happens to make the denominator of the identity equal to 0.

Double angles

In each case, use one of the Double Angle Formulas.

To find the sine or cosine of twice a known angle, use one of the following formulas:

$$\sin(2\theta) = 2\sin\theta\cos\theta$$

$$\cos(2\theta) = \cos^2\theta - \sin^2\theta \quad \text{or}$$

$$\cos(2\theta) = 2\cos^2\theta - 1 \quad \text{or}$$

$$\cos(2\theta) = 1 - 2\sin^2\theta$$

To find the tangent or cotangent of twice a known angle, use the formulas:

$$\tan(2\theta) = \frac{2\tan\theta}{1-\tan^2\theta}$$

$$\cot(2\theta) = \frac{\cot\theta - \tan\theta}{2}$$

In each case, θ is an angle with known exact sine, cosine, tangent, and cotangent values.

Products

To find the product of the sines and cosines of two different angles, use one of the following formulas:

$$\sin\alpha\sin\beta = \frac{1}{2}[\cos(\alpha - \beta) - \cos(\alpha + \beta)]$$

$$\cos\alpha\cos\beta = \frac{1}{2}[\cos(\alpha + \beta) + \cos(\alpha - \beta)]$$

$$\sin\alpha\cos\beta = \frac{1}{2}[\sin(\alpha + \beta) + \sin(\alpha - \beta)]$$

$$\cos\alpha\sin\beta = \frac{1}{2}[\sin(\alpha + \beta) - \sin(\alpha - \beta)]$$

where α and β are two unique angles.

Complementary

The trigonometric cofunction identities use the trigonometric relationships of complementary angles (angles whose sum is 90°). These are:

$$\cos x = \sin(90° - x)$$
$$\csc x = \sec(90° - x)$$
$$\cot x = \tan(90° - x)$$

Pythagorean

The Pythagorean Theorem states that $a^2 + b^2 = c^2$ for all right triangles. The trigonometric identity that derives from this principles is stated in this way:

$$\sin^2\theta + \cos^2\theta = 1$$

Dividing each term by either $\sin^2\theta$ or $\cos^2\theta$ yields two other identities, respectively:

$$1 + \cot^2 \theta = \csc^2 \theta$$

$$\tan^2 \theta + 1 = \sec^2 \theta$$

Unit Circle

A unit circle is a circle with a radius of 1 that has its center at the origin. The equation of the unit circle is $x^2 + y^2 = 1$. Notice that this is an abbreviated version of the standard equation of a circle. Because the center is the point $(0, 0)$, the values of h and k in the general equation are equal to zero and the equation simplifies to this form.

Standard Position: The position of an angle of measure θ whose vertex is at the origin, the initial side crosses the unit circle at the point $(1, 0)$, and the terminal side crosses the unit circle at some other point (a, b). In the standard position, $\sin \theta = b$, $\cos \theta = a$, and $\tan \theta = \frac{b}{a}$.

Rectangular coordinates are those that lie on the square grids of the Cartesian plane. They should be quite familiar to you. The polar coordinate system is based on a circular graph, rather than the square grid of the Cartesian system. Points in the polar coordinate system are in the format (r, θ), where r is the distance from the origin (think radius of the circle) and θ is the smallest positive angle (moving counterclockwise around the circle) made with the positive horizontal axis.

To convert a point from rectangular (x, y) format to polar (r, θ) format, use the formula (x, y) to $(r, \theta) \Rightarrow r = \sqrt{x^2 + y^2}$; $\theta = \arctan \frac{y}{x}$ when $x \neq 0$

If x is positive, use the positive square root value for r. If x is negative, use the negative square root value for r.

If x = 0, use the following rules:

If x = 0 and y = 0, then $\theta = 0$

If x = 0 and y > 0, then $\theta = \frac{\pi}{2}$

If x = 0 and y < 0, then $\theta = \frac{3\pi}{2}$

To convert a point from polar (r, θ) format to rectangular (x, y) format, use the formula (r, θ) to $(x, y) \Rightarrow x = r \cos \theta \, ; y = r \sin \theta$

Table of commonly encountered angles

$0° = 0$ radians, $30° = \frac{\pi}{6}$ radians, $45° = \frac{\pi}{4}$ radians, $60° = \frac{\pi}{3}$ radians, and $90° = \frac{\pi}{2}$ radians

$\sin 0° = 0$	$\cos 0° = 1$	$\tan 0° = 0$
$\sin 30° = \frac{1}{2}$	$\cos 30° = \frac{\sqrt{3}}{2}$	$\tan 30° = \frac{\sqrt{3}}{3}$
$\sin 45° = \frac{\sqrt{2}}{2}$	$\cos 45° = \frac{\sqrt{2}}{2}$	$\tan 45° = 1$
$\sin 60° = \frac{\sqrt{3}}{2}$	$\cos 60° = \frac{1}{2}$	$\tan 60° = \sqrt{3}$
$\sin 90° = 1$	$\cos 90° = 0$	$\tan 90° =$ undefined
$\csc 0° =$ undefined	$\sec 0° = 1$	$\cot 0° =$ undefined
$\csc 30° = 2$	$\sec 30° = \frac{2\sqrt{3}}{3}$	$\cot 30° = \sqrt{3}$
$\csc 45° = \sqrt{2}$	$\sec 45° = \sqrt{2}$	$\cot 45° = 1$
$\csc 60° = \frac{2\sqrt{3}}{3}$	$\sec 60° = 2$	$\cot 60° = \frac{\sqrt{3}}{3}$
$\csc 90° = 1$	$\sec 90° =$ undefined	$\cot 90° = 0$

The values in the upper half of this table are values you should have memorized or be able to find quickly.

Sequences and Series

A sequence is a set of numbers that continues on in a define pattern. The function that defines a sequence has a domain composed of the set of positive integers. Each member of the sequence is an element, or individual term. Each element is identified by the notation a_n, where a is the term of the sequence, and n is the integer identifying which term in the sequence a is. There are two different ways to represent a sequence that contains the element a_n. The first is the simple notation $\{a_n\}$. The expanded notation of a sequence is $a_1, a_2, a_3, \ldots a_n, \ldots$. Notice that the expanded form does not end with the nth term. There is no indication that the nth term is the last term in the sequence, only that the nth term is an element of the sequence.

Some sequences will have a limit, or a value the sequence approaches or sometimes even reaches but never passes. A sequence that has a limit is known as a convergent sequence because all the values of the sequence seemingly converge at that point. Sequences that do not converge at a particular limit are divergent sequences. The easiest way to determine whether a sequence converges or diverges is to find the limit of the sequence. If the limit is a real number, the sequence is a convergent sequence. If the limit is infinity, the sequence is a divergent sequence. Remember the following rules for finding limits:

$\lim_{n \to \infty} k = k$ for all real numbers k

$\lim_{n \to \infty} \frac{1}{n} = 0$

$\lim_{n \to \infty} n = \infty$

$\lim_{n \to \infty} \frac{k}{n^p} = 0$ for all real numbers k and positive rational numbers p.

The limit of the sums of two sequences is equal to the sum of the limits of the two sequences: $\lim_{n \to \infty}(a_n + b_n) = \lim_{n \to \infty} a_n + \lim_{n \to \infty} b_n$.

The limit of the difference between two sequences is equal to the difference between the limits of the two sequences:

$\lim_{n \to \infty}(a_n - b_n) = \lim_{n \to \infty} a_n - \lim_{n \to \infty} b_n$.

The limit of the product of two sequences is equal to the product of the limits of the two sequences: $\lim_{n \to \infty}(a_n \cdot b_n) = \lim_{n \to \infty} a_n \cdot \lim_{n \to \infty} b_n$.

The limit of the quotient of two sequences is equal to the quotient of the limits of the two sequences, with some exceptions: $\lim_{n \to \infty}\left(\frac{a_n}{b_n}\right) = \frac{\lim_{n \to \infty} a_n}{\lim_{n \to \infty} b_n}$. In the quotient formula, it is important to consider that $b_n \neq 0$ and $\lim_{n \to \infty} b_n \neq 0$.

The limit of a sequence multiplied by a scalar is equal to the scalar multiplied by the limit of the sequence: $\lim_{n \to \infty} k a_n = k \lim_{n \to \infty} a_n$, where k is any real number.

A **monotonic sequence** is a sequence that is either nonincreasing or nondecreasing. The term *nonincreasing* is used to describe a sequence whose terms either get progressively smaller in value or remain the same. The term *nondecreasing* is used to describe a sequence whose terms either get progressively larger in value or remain the same. A nonincreasing sequence is bounded above. This means that all elements of the sequence must be less than a given real number. A nondecreasing sequence is bounded below. This means that all elements of the sequence must be greater than a given real number.

Whenever one element of a sequence is defined in terms of a previous element or elements of the sequence, the sequence is a **recursive sequence**. For example, given the recursive definition $a_1 = 0$; $a_2 = 1$; $a_n = a_{n-1} + a_{n-2}$ for all $n \geq 2$, you get the sequence 0, 1, 1, 2, 3, 5, 8, ... This particular sequence is known as the Fibonacci sequence, and is defined as the numbers zero and one, and a continuing sequence of numbers, with each number in the sequence equal to the sum of the two previous numbers. It is important to note that the Fibonacci sequence can also be defined as the first two terms being equal to one, with the remaining terms equal to the sum of the previous two terms. Both definitions are considered correct in mathematics.

Make sure you know which definition you are working with when dealing with Fibonacci numbers.

Sometimes one term of a sequence with a recursive definition can be found without knowing the previous terms of the sequence. This case is known as a closed-form expression for a recursive definition. In this case, an alternate formula will apply to the sequence to generate the same sequence of numbers. However, not all sequences based on recursive definitions will have a closed-form expression. Some sequences will require the use of the recursive definition. For example, the Fibonacci sequence has a closed-form expression given by the formula $a_n = \frac{\phi^n - \left(\frac{-1}{\phi}\right)^n}{\sqrt{5}}$, where φ is the golden ratio, which is equal to $\frac{1+\sqrt{5}}{2}$. In this case, $a_0 = 0$ and $a_1 = 1$, so you know which definition of the Fibonacci sequence you have.

An **arithmetic sequence**, or arithmetic progression, is a special kind of sequence in which each term has a specific quantity, called the common difference, that is added to the previous term. The common difference may be positive or negative. The general form of an arithmetic sequence containing n terms is $a_1, a_1 + d, a_1 + 2d, \dots, a_1 + (n-1)d$, where d is the common difference. The formula for the general term of an arithmetic sequence is $a_n = a_1 + (n-1)d$, where a_n is the term you are looking for and d is the common difference. To find the sum of the first n terms of an arithmetic sequence, use the formula $S_n = \frac{n}{2}(a_1 + a_n)$.

A **geometric sequence**, or geometric progression, is a special kind of sequence in which each term has a specific quantity, called the common ratio, multiplied by the previous term. The common ratio may be positive or negative. The general form of a geometric sequence containing n terms is $a_1, a_1 r, a_1 r^2, \dots, a_1 r^{n-1}$, where r is the common ratio. The formula for the general term of a geometric sequence is $a_n = a_1 r^{n-1}$, where a_n is the term you are looking for and r is the common ratio. To

find the sum of the first n terms of a geometric sequence, use the formula
$S_n = \frac{a_1(1-r^n)}{1-r}$.

Any function with the set of all natural numbers as the domain is also called a sequence. An element of a sequence is denoted by the symbol a_n, which represents the nth element of sequence a. Sequences may be arithmetic or geometric, and may be defined by a recursive definition, closed-form expression or both. Arithmetic and geometric sequences both have recursive definitions based on the first term of the sequence, as well as both having formulas to find the sum of the first n terms in the sequence, assuming you know what the first term is. The sum of all the terms in a sequence is called a **series**.

An infinite series, also referred to as just a series, is a series of partial sums of a defined sequence. Each infinite sequence represents an infinite series according to the equation $\sum_{n=1}^{\infty} a_n = a_1 + a_2 + a_3 + \cdots + a_n + \cdots$. This notation can be shortened to $\sum_{n=1}^{\infty} a_n$ or $\sum a_n$. Every series is a sequence of partial sums, where the first partial sum is equal to the first element of the series, the second partial sum is equal to the sum of the first two elements of the series, and the nth partial sum is equal to the sum of the first n elements of the series.

Every infinite sequence of partial sums either converges or diverges. Like the test for convergence in a sequence, finding the limit of the sequence of partial sums will indicate whether it is a converging series or a diverging series. If there exists a real number S such that $\lim_{n \to \infty} S_n = S$, where S_n is the sequence of partial sums, then the series converges. If the limit equals infinity, then the series diverges. If $\lim_{n \to \infty} S_n = S$ and S is a real number, then S is also the convergence value of the series.

To find the sum as n approaches infinity for the sum of two convergent series, find the sum as n approaches infinity for each individual series and add the results.

$$\sum_{n=1}^{\infty} (a_n + b_n) = \sum_{n=1}^{\infty} a_n + \sum_{n=1}^{\infty} b_n$$

To find the sum as n approaches infinity for the difference between two convergent series, find the sum as n approaches infinity for each individual series and subtract the results.

$$\sum_{n=1}^{\infty} (a_n - b_n) = \sum_{n=1}^{\infty} a_n - \sum_{n=1}^{\infty} b_n$$

To find the sum as n approaches infinity for the product of a scalar and a convergent series, find the sum as n approaches infinity for the series and multiply the result by the scalar.

$$\sum_{n=1}^{\infty} k a_n = k \sum_{n=1}^{\infty} a_n$$

A **geometric series** is an infinite series in which each term is multiplied by a constant real number r, called the ratio. This is represented by the equation

$$\sum_{n=1}^{\infty} ar^{n-1} = a_1 + a_2 r + a_3 r^2 + \cdots + a_n r^{n-1} + \cdots$$

If the absolute value of r is greater than or equal to one, then the geometric series is a diverging series. If the absolute value of r is less than one but greater than zero, the geometric series is a converging series. To find the sum of a converging geometric series, use the formula

$$\sum_{n=1}^{\infty} ar^{n-1} = \frac{a}{1-r}, \text{where } 0 < |r| < 1$$

The **n^{th} term test for divergence** involves taking the limit of the nth term of a sequence and determining whether or not the limit is equal to zero. If the limit of the nth term is not equal to zero, then the series is a diverging series. This test only works to prove divergence, however. If the nth term is equal to zero, the test is inconclusive.

Reading Comprehension Test

Important Skills

One of the most important skills in reading comprehension is the identification of **topics** and **main ideas.** There is a subtle difference between these two features. The topic is the subject of a text, or what the text is about. The main idea, on the other hand, is the most important point being made by the author. The topic is usually expressed in a few words at the most, while the main idea often needs a full sentence to be completely defined. As an example, a short passage might have the topic of penguins and the main idea *Penguins are different from other birds in many ways.* In most nonfiction writing, the topic and the main idea will be stated directly, often in a sentence at the very beginning or end of the text. When being tested on an understanding of the author's topic, the reader can quickly *skim* the passage for the general idea, stopping to read only the first sentence of each paragraph. A paragraph's first sentence is often (but not always) the main topic sentence, and it gives you a summary of the content of the paragraph. However, there are cases in which the reader must figure out an unstated topic or main idea. In these instances, the student must read every sentence of the text, and try to come up with an overarching idea that is supported by each of those sentences.

While the main idea is the overall premise of a story, **supporting details** provide evidence and backing for the main point. In order to show that a main idea is correct, or valid, the author needs to add details that prove their point. All texts contain details, but they are only classified as supporting details when they serve to reinforce some larger point. Supporting details are most commonly found in informative and persuasive texts. In some cases, they will be clearly indicated with words like *for example* or *for instance*, or they will be enumerated with words like *first, second,* and *last.* However, they may not be indicated with special words. As a reader, it is important to consider whether the author's supporting details really back up his or her main point. Supporting details can be factual and correct but still not relevant to the author's point. Conversely, supporting details can seem pertinent but be ineffective because they are based on opinion or assertions that cannot be proven.

An example of a main idea is: "Giraffes live in the Serengeti of Africa." A supporting detail about giraffes could be: "A giraffe uses its long neck to reach twigs and leaves on trees." The main idea gives the general idea that the text is about giraffes. The supporting detail gives a specific fact about how the giraffes eat.

As opposed to a main idea, themes are seldom expressed directly in a text, so they can be difficult to identify. A **theme** is an issue, an idea, or a question raised by the text. For instance, a theme of William Shakespeare's *Hamlet* is indecision, as the title character explores his own psyche and the results of his failure to make bold choices. A great work of literature may have many themes, and the reader is justified in identifying any for which he or she can find support. One common characteristic of themes is that they raise more questions than they answer. In a good piece of fiction, the author is not always trying to convince the reader, but is instead trying to elevate the reader's perspective and encourage him to consider the themes more deeply. When reading, one can identify themes by constantly asking what general issues the text is addressing. A good way to evaluate an author's approach to a theme is to begin reading with a question in mind (for example, how does this text approach the theme of love?) and then look for evidence in the text that addresses that question.

Purposes for Writing

In order to be an effective reader, one must pay attention to the author's **position** and purpose. Even those texts that seem objective and impartial, like textbooks, have some sort of position and bias. Readers need to take these positions into account when considering the author's message. When an author uses emotional language or clearly favors one side of an argument, his position is clear. However, the author's position may be evident not only in what he writes, but in what he doesn't write. For this reason, it is sometimes necessary to review some other texts on the same topic in order to develop a view of the author's position. If this is not possible, then it may be useful to acquire a little background personal information about the author. When the only source of information is the text, however, the reader should look for language and argumentation that seems to indicate a particular stance on the subject.

Identifying the **purpose** of an author is usually easier than identifying her position. In most cases, the author has no interest in hiding his or her purpose. A text that is meant to entertain, for instance, should be obviously written to please the reader. Most narratives, or stories, are written to entertain, though they may also inform or persuade. Informative texts are easy to identify as well. The most difficult purpose of a text to identify is persuasion, because the author has an interest in making this purpose hard to detect. When a person knows that the author is trying to convince him, he is automatically more wary and skeptical of the argument. For this reason persuasive texts often try to establish an entertaining tone, hoping to amuse the reader into agreement, or an informative tone, hoping to create an appearance of authority and objectivity.

An author's purpose is often evident in the organization of the text. For instance, if the text has headings and subheadings, if key terms are in bold, and if the author makes his main idea clear from the beginning, then the likely purpose of the text is to inform. If the author begins by making a claim and then makes various arguments to support that claim, the purpose is probably to persuade. If the author is telling a story, or is more interested in holding the attention of the reader than in making a particular point or delivering information, then his purpose is most likely to entertain. As a reader, it is best to judge an author on how well he accomplishes his purpose. In other words, it is not entirely fair to complain that a textbook is boring: if the text is clear and easy to understand, then the author has done his job.

Similarly, a storyteller should not be judged too harshly for getting some facts wrong, so long as he is able to give pleasure to the reader.

The author's purpose for writing will affect his writing style and the response of the reader. In a **persuasive essay**, the author is attempting to change the reader's mind or convince him of something he did not believe previously. There are several identifying characteristics of persuasive writing. One is opinion presented as fact. When an author attempts to persuade the reader, he often presents his or her opinions as if they were fact. A reader must be on guard for statements that sound factual but which cannot be subjected to research, observation, or experiment. Another characteristic of persuasive writing is emotional language. An author will often try to play on the reader's emotion by appealing to his sympathy or sense of morality. When an author uses colorful or evocative language with the intent of arousing the reader's passions, it is likely that he is attempting to persuade. Finally, in many cases a persuasive text will give an unfair explanation of opposing positions, if these positions are mentioned at all.

An **informative text** is written to educate and enlighten the reader. Informative texts are almost always nonfiction, and are rarely structured as a story. The intention of an informative text is to deliver information in the most comprehensible way possible, so the structure of the text is likely to be very clear. In an informative text, the thesis statement is often in the first sentence. The author may use some colorful language, but is likely to put more emphasis on clarity and precision. Informative essays do not typically appeal to the emotions. They often contain facts and figures, and rarely include the opinion of the author. Sometimes a persuasive essay can resemble an informative essay, especially if the author maintains an even tone and presents his or her views as if they were established fact.

The success or failure of an author's intent to **entertain** is determined by those who read the author's work. Entertaining texts may be either fiction or nonfiction, and they may describe real or imagined people, places, and events. Entertaining texts are often narratives, or stories. A text that is written to entertain is likely to contain colorful language that engages the imagination and the emotions. Such writing often features a great deal of figurative language, which typically enlivens its subject matter with images and analogies. Though an entertaining text is not usually written to persuade or inform, it may accomplish both of these tasks. An entertaining text may appeal to the reader's emotions and cause him or her to think differently about a particular subject. In any case, entertaining texts tend to showcase the personality of the author more so than do other types of writing.

When an author intends to **express feelings,** she may use colorful and evocative language. An author may write emotionally for any number of reasons. Sometimes, the author will do so because she is describing a personal situation of great pain or happiness. Sometimes an author is attempting to persuade the reader, and so will use emotion to stir up the passions. It can be easy to identify this kind of expression when the writer uses phrases like *I felt* and *I sense*. However, sometimes the author will simply describe feelings without introducing them. As a reader, it is important to recognize when an author is expressing emotion, and not to become overwhelmed by sympathy or passion. A reader should maintain some detachment so that he or she can still evaluate the strength of the author's argument or the quality of the writing.

In a sense, almost all writing is descriptive, insofar as it seeks to describe events, ideas, or people to the reader. Some texts, however, are primarily concerned with **description**. A descriptive text focuses on a particular subject, and attempts to depict it in a way that will be clear to the reader. Descriptive texts contain many adjectives and adverbs, words that give shades of meaning and create a more detailed mental picture for the reader. A descriptive text fails when it is unclear or vague to the reader. On the other hand, however, a descriptive text that compiles too much detail can be boring and overwhelming to the reader. A descriptive text will certainly be informative, and it may be persuasive and entertaining as well.

Descriptive writing is a challenge for the author, but when it is done well, it can be fun to read.

Writing Devices

Authors will use different stylistic and writing devices to make their meaning more clearly understood. One of those devices is comparison and contrast. When an author describes the ways in which two things are alike, he or she is **comparing** them. When the author describes the ways in which two things are different, he or she is **contrasting** them. The "compare and contrast" essay is one of the most common forms in nonfiction. It is often signaled with certain words: a comparison may be indicated with such words as *both, same, like, too,* and *as well*; while a contrast may be indicated by words like *but, however, on the other hand, instead,* and *yet*. Of course, comparisons and contrasts may be implicit without using any such signaling language. A single sentence may both compare and contrast. Consider the sentence *Brian and Sheila love ice cream, but Brian prefers vanilla and Sheila prefers strawberry.* In one sentence, the author has described both a similarity (love of ice cream) and a difference (favorite flavor).

One of the most common text structures is **cause and effect**. A cause is an act or event that makes something happen, and an effect is the thing that happens as a result of that cause. A cause-and-effect relationship is not always explicit, but there are some words in English that signal causality, such as *since, because,* and *as a result*. As an example, consider the sentence *Because the sky was clear, Ron did not bring an umbrella.* The cause is the clear sky, and the effect is that Ron did not bring an umbrella. However, sometimes the cause-and-effect relationship will not be clearly noted. For instance, the sentence *He was late and missed the meeting* does not contain any signaling words, but it still contains a cause (he was late) and an effect (he missed the meeting). It is possible for a single cause to have multiple effects, or for a single effect to have multiple causes. Also, an effect can in turn be the cause of another effect, in what is known as a cause-and-effect chain.

Authors often use analogies to add meaning to the text. An **analogy** is a comparison of two things. The words in the analogy are connected by a certain, often undetermined relationship. Look at this analogy: moo is to cow as quack is to duck. This analogy compares the sound that a cow makes with the sound that a duck makes. Even if the word 'quack' was not given, one could figure out it is the correct word to complete the analogy based on the relationship between the words 'moo' and 'cow'. Some common relationships for analogies include synonyms, antonyms, part to whole, definition, and actor to action.

Another element that impacts a text is the author's point of view. The **point of view** of a text is the perspective from which it is told. The author will always have a point of view about a story before he draws up a plot line. The author will know what events they want to take place, how they want the characters to interact, and how the story will resolve. An author will also have an opinion on the topic, or series of events, which is presented in the story, based on their own prior experience and beliefs.

The two main points of view that authors use are first person and third person. If the narrator of the story is also the main character, or *protagonist*, the text is written in first-person point of view. In first person, the author writes with the word *I*. Third-person point of view is probably the most common point of view that authors use. Using third person, authors refer to each character using the words *he* or *she*. In third-person omniscient, the narrator is not a character in the story and tells the story of all of the characters at the same time.

A good writer will use **transitional words** and phrases to guide the reader through the text. You are no doubt familiar with the common transitions, though you may never have considered how they operate. Some transitional phrases (*after, before, during, in the middle of*) give information about time. Some indicate that an example is about to be given (*for example, in fact, for instance*). Writers use them to compare (*also, likewise*) and contrast (*however, but, yet*). Transitional words and phrases can suggest addition (*and, also, furthermore, moreover*) and logical relationships (*if, then, therefore, as a result, since*). Finally, transitional words and phrases can demarcate the steps in a process (*first, second, last*). You should incorporate transitional words and phrases where they will orient your reader and illuminate the structure of your composition.

Types of Passages

A **narrative** passage is a story. Narratives can be fiction or nonfiction. However, there are a few elements that a text must have in order to be classified as a narrative. To begin with, the text must have a plot. That is, it must describe a series of events. If it is a good narrative, these events will be interesting and emotionally engaging to the reader. A narrative also has characters. These could be people, animals, or even inanimate objects, so long as they participate in the plot. A narrative passage often contains figurative language, which is meant to stimulate the imagination of the reader by making comparisons and observations. A metaphor, which is a description of one thing in terms of another, is a common piece of figurative language. *The moon was a frosty snowball* is an example of a metaphor: it is obviously untrue in the literal sense, but it suggests a certain mood for the reader. Narratives often proceed in a clear sequence, but they do not need to do so.

An **expository** passage aims to inform and enlighten the reader. It is nonfiction and usually centers around a simple, easily defined topic. Since the goal of exposition is to teach, such a passage should be as clear as possible. It is common for an expository passage to contain helpful organizing words, like *first, next, for example,* and *therefore*. These words keep the reader oriented in the text. Although expository passages do not need to feature colorful language and artful writing, they are often more effective when they do. For a reader, the challenge of expository passages is to maintain steady attention. Expository passages are not always about subjects in which a reader will naturally be interested, and the writer is often more concerned with clarity and comprehensibility than with engaging the reader. For this reason, many expository passages are dull. Making notes is a good way to maintain focus when reading an expository passage.

A **technical** passage is written to describe a complex object or process. Technical writing is common in medical and technological fields, in which complicated mathematical, scientific, and engineering ideas need to be explained simply and clearly. To ease comprehension, a technical passage usually proceeds in a very logical order. Technical passages often have clear headings and subheadings, which are used to keep the reader oriented in the text. It is also common for these passages to break sections up with numbers or letters. Many technical passages look more like an outline than a piece of prose. The amount of jargon or difficult vocabulary will vary in a technical passage depending on the intended audience. As much as possible, technical passages try to avoid language that the reader will have to research in order to understand the message. Of course, it is not always possible to avoid jargon.

A **persuasive** passage is meant to change the reader's mind or lead her into agreement with the author. The persuasive intent may be obvious, or it may be quite difficult to discern. In some cases, a persuasive passage will be indistinguishable from an informative passage: it will make an assertion and offer supporting details. However, a persuasive passage is more likely to make claims based on opinion and to appeal to the reader's emotions. Persuasive passages may not describe alternate positions and, when they do, they often display significant bias. It may be clear that a persuasive passage is giving the author's viewpoint, or the passage may adopt a seemingly objective tone. A persuasive passage is successful if it can make a convincing argument and win the trust of the reader.

A persuasive essay will likely focus on one central argument, but it may make many smaller claims along the way. These are subordinate arguments with which the reader must agree if he or she is going to agree with the central argument. The central argument will only be as strong as the subordinate claims. These claims should be rooted in fact and observation, rather than subjective judgment. The best persuasive essays provide enough supporting detail to justify claims without overwhelming the reader. Remember that a fact must be susceptible to independent verification: that is, it must be something the reader could confirm. Also, statistics are only effective when they take into account possible objections. For instance, a statistic on the number of foreclosed houses would only be useful if it was taken over a defined interval and in a defined area. Most readers are wary of statistics, because they are so often misleading. If possible, a persuasive essay should always include references so that the reader can obtain more information. Of course, this means that the writer's accuracy and fairness may be judged by the inquiring reader.

Opinions are formed by emotion as well as reason, and persuasive writers often appeal to the feelings of the reader. Although readers should always be skeptical of this technique, it is often used in a proper and ethical manner. For instance, there are many subjects that have an obvious emotional component, and therefore cannot be completely treated without an appeal to the emotions. Consider an article on drunk driving: it makes sense to include some specific examples that will alarm or sadden the reader. After all, drunk driving often has serious and tragic consequences. Emotional appeals are not appropriate, however, when they attempt to mislead the reader. For instance, in political advertisements it is common to emphasize the patriotism of the preferred candidate, because this will encourage the audience to link their own positive feelings about the country with their opinion of the candidate. However, these ads often imply that the other candidate is unpatriotic, which in most cases is far from the truth. Another common and improper emotional appeal is the use of loaded language, as for instance referring to an avidly religious person as a "fanatic" or a passionate environmentalist as a "tree hugger." These terms introduce an emotional component that detracts from the argument.

History and Culture

Historical context has a profound influence on literature: the events, knowledge base, and assumptions of an author's time color every aspect of his or her work. Sometimes, authors hold opinions and use language that would be considered inappropriate or immoral in a modern setting, but that was acceptable in the author's time. As a reader, one should consider how the historical context influenced a work and also how today's opinions and ideas shape the way modern readers read the works of the past. For instance, in most societies of the past, women were treated as second-class citizens. An author who wrote in 18th-century England might sound sexist to modern readers, even if that author was relatively feminist in his time. Readers should not have to excuse the faulty assumptions and prejudices of the past, but they should appreciate that a person's thoughts and words are, in part, a result of the time and culture in which they live or lived, and it is perhaps unfair to expect writers to avoid all of the errors of their times.

Even a brief study of world literature suggests that writers from vastly different cultures address similar themes. For instance, works like the *Odyssey* and *Hamlet* both tackle the individual's battle for self-control and independence. In every culture, authors address themes of personal growth and the struggle for maturity. Another universal theme is the conflict between the individual and society. In works as culturally disparate as *Native Son*, the *Aeneid*, and *1984*, authors dramatize how people struggle to maintain their personalities and dignity in large, sometimes oppressive groups. Finally, many cultures have versions of the hero's (or heroine's) journey, in which an adventurous person must overcome many obstacles in order to gain greater knowledge, power, and perspective. Some famous works that treat this theme are the *Epic of Gilgamesh*, Dante's *Divine Comedy*, and *Don Quixote*.

Authors from different genres (for instance poetry, drama, novel, short story) and cultures may address similar themes, but they often do so quite differently. For instance, poets are likely to address subject matter obliquely, through the use of images and allusions. In a play, on the other hand, the author is more likely to dramatize themes by using characters to express opposing viewpoints. This disparity is known as a dialectical approach. In a novel, the author does not need to express themes directly; rather, they can be illustrated through events and actions. In some regional literatures, like those of Greece or England, authors use more irony: their works have characters that express views and make decisions that are clearly disapproved of by the author. In Latin America, there is a great tradition of using supernatural events to illustrate themes about real life. In China and Japan, authors frequently use well-established regional forms (haiku, for instance) to organize their treatment of universal themes.

Responding to Literature

When reading good literature, the reader is moved to engage actively in the text. One part of being an active reader involves making predictions. A **prediction** is a guess about what will happen next. Readers are constantly making predictions based on what they have read and what they already know. Consider the following sentence: *Staring at the computer screen in shock, Kim blindly reached over for the brimming glass of water on the shelf to her side.* The sentence suggests that Kim is agitated and that she is not looking at the glass she is going to pick up, so a reader might predict that she is going to knock the glass over. Of course, not every prediction will be accurate: perhaps Kim will pick the glass up cleanly. Nevertheless, the author has certainly created the expectation that the water might be spilled. Predictions are always subject to revision as the reader acquires more information.

Test-taking tip: To respond to questions requiring future predictions, the student's answers should be based on evidence of past or present behavior.

Readers are often required to understand text that claims and suggests ideas without stating them directly. An **inference** is a piece of information that is implied but not written outright by the author. For instance, consider the following sentence: *Mark made more money that week than he had in the previous year*. From this sentence, the reader can infer that Mark either has not made much money in the previous year or made a great deal of money that week. Often, a reader can use information he or she already knows to make inferences. Take as an example the sentence *When his coffee arrived, he looked around the table for the silver cup*. Many people know that cream is typically served in a silver cup, so using their own base of knowledge they can infer that the subject of this sentence takes his coffee with cream. Making inferences requires concentration, attention, and practice.

Test-taking tip: While being tested on his ability to make correct inferences, the student must look for contextual clues. An answer can be *true* but not *correct*. The contextual clues will help you find the answer that is the best answer out of the given choices. Understand the context in which a phrase is stated. When asked for the implied meaning of a statement made in the passage, the student should immediately locate the statement and read the context in which it was made. Also, look for an answer choice that has a similar phrase to the statement in question.

A reader must be able to identify a text's **sequence**, or the order in which things happen. Often, and especially when the sequence is very important to the author, it is indicated with signal words like *first, then, next,* and *last*. However, sometimes a sequence is merely implied and must be noted by the reader. Consider the sentence *He walked in the front door and switched on the hall lamp*. Clearly, the man did not turn the lamp on before he walked in the door, so the implied sequence is that he first walked in the door and then turned on the lamp. Texts do not always proceed in an orderly sequence from first to last: sometimes, they begin at the end and then start over at the beginning. As a reader, it can be useful to make brief notes to clarify the sequence.

In addition to inferring and predicting things about the text, the reader must often **draw conclusions** about the information he has read. When asked for a *conclusion* that may be drawn, look for critical "hedge" phrases, such as *likely, may, can, will* *often*, among many others. When you are being tested on this knowledge, remember that question writers insert these hedge phrases to cover every possibility. Often an answer will be wrong simply because it leaves no room for exception. Extreme positive or negative answers (such as always, never, etc.) are usually not correct. The reader should not use any outside knowledge that is not gathered from the reading passage to answer the related questions. Correct answers can be derived straight from the reading passage.

Opinions, Facts, & Fallacies

Critical thinking skills are mastered through understanding various types of writing and the different purposes that authors have for writing the way they do. Every author writes for a purpose. Understanding that purpose, and how they accomplish their goal, will allow you to critique the writing and determine whether or not you agree with their conclusions.

Readers must always be conscious of the distinction between fact and opinion. A **fact** can be subjected to analysis and can be either proved or disproved. An **opinion**, on the other hand, is the author's personal feeling, which may not be alterable by research, evidence, or argument. If the author writes that the distance from New York to Boston is about two hundred miles, he is stating a fact. But if he writes that New York is too crowded, then he is giving an opinion, because there is no objective standard for overpopulation. An opinion may be indicated by words like *believe*, *think*, or *feel*. Also, an opinion may be supported by facts: for instance, the author might give the population density of New York as a reason for why it is overcrowded. An opinion supported by fact tends to be more convincing. When authors support their opinions with other opinions, the reader is unlikely to be moved.

Facts should be presented to the reader from reliable sources. An opinion is what the author thinks about a given topic. An opinion is not common knowledge or proven by expert sources, but it is information that the author believes and wants the reader to consider. To distinguish between fact and opinion, a reader needs to look at the type of source that is presenting information, what information backs-up a claim, and whether or not the author may be motivated to have a certain point of view on a given topic. For example, if a panel of scientists has conducted multiple studies on the effectiveness of taking a certain vitamin, the results are more likely to be factual than if a company selling a vitamin claims that taking the vitamin can produce positive effects. The company is motivated to sell its product, while the scientists are using the scientific method to prove a theory. If the author uses words such as "I think…", the statement is an opinion.

In their attempt to persuade, writers often make mistakes in their thinking patterns and writing choices. It's important to understand these so you can make an informed decision. Every author has a point of view, but when an author ignores reasonable counterarguments or distorts opposing viewpoints, she is demonstrating a **bias**. A bias is evident whenever the author is unfair or inaccurate in his or her presentation. Bias may be intentional or unintentional, but it should always alert the reader to be skeptical of the argument being made. It should be noted that a biased author may still be correct. However, the author will be correct in spite of her bias, not because of it. A **stereotype** is like a bias, except that it is specifically applied to a group or place. Stereotyping is considered to be particularly abhorrent because it promotes negative generalizations about people. Many people are familiar with some of the hateful stereotypes of certain ethnic, religious, and cultural groups. Readers should be very wary of authors who stereotype. These faulty assumptions typically reveal the author's ignorance and lack of curiosity.

Sometimes, authors will **appeal to the reader's emotion** in an attempt to persuade or to distract the reader from the weakness of the argument. For instance, the author may try to inspire the pity of the reader by delivering a heart-rending story. An author also might use the bandwagon approach, in which he suggests that his opinion is correct because it is held by the majority. Some authors resort to name-calling, in which insults and harsh words are delivered to the opponent in an attempt to distract. In advertising, a common appeal is the testimonial, in which a famous person endorses a product. Of course, the fact that a celebrity likes something should not really mean anything to the reader. These and other emotional appeals are usually evidence of poor reasoning and a weak argument.

Certain *logical fallacies* are frequent in writing. A logical fallacy is a failure of reasoning. As a reader, it is important to recognize logical fallacies, because they diminish the value of the author's message. The four most common logical fallacies in writing are the false analogy, circular reasoning, false dichotomy, and overgeneralization. In a **false analogy**, the author suggests that two things are similar, when in fact they are different. This fallacy is often committed when the author is attempting to convince the reader that something unknown is like something relatively familiar. The author takes advantage of the reader's ignorance to make this false comparison. One example might be the following statement: *Failing to tip a waitress is like stealing money out of somebody's wallet.* Of course, failing to tip is very rude, especially when the service has been good, but people are not arrested for failing to tip as they would for stealing money from a wallet. To compare stingy diners with thieves is a false analogy.

Circular reasoning is one of the more difficult logical fallacies to identify, because it is typically hidden behind dense language and complicated sentences. Reasoning is described as circular when it offers no support for assertions other than restating them in different words. Put another way, a circular argument refers to itself as evidence of truth. A simple example of circular argument is when a person uses a word to define itself, such as saying *Niceness is the state of being nice.* If the reader does not know what *nice* means, then this definition will not be very useful. In a text, circular reasoning is usually more complex. For instance, an author might say *Poverty is a problem for society because it creates trouble for people throughout the community.* It is redundant to say that poverty is a problem because it creates trouble. When an author engages in circular reasoning, it is often because he or she has not fully thought out the argument, or cannot come up with any legitimate justifications.

One of the most common logical fallacies is the **false dichotomy**, in which the author creates an artificial sense that there are only two possible alternatives in a situation. This fallacy is common when the author has an agenda and wants to give the impression that his view is the only sensible one. A false dichotomy has the effect of limiting the reader's options and imagination. An example of a false dichotomy is the statement *You need to go to the party with me, otherwise you'll just be bored at home.* The speaker suggests that the only other possibility besides being at the party is being bored at home. But this is not true, as it is perfectly possible to be entertained at home, or even to go somewhere other than the party. Readers should always be wary of the false dichotomy: when an author limits alternatives, it is always wise to ask whether he is being valid.

Overgeneralization is a logical fallacy in which the author makes a claim that is so broad it cannot be proved or disproved. In most cases, overgeneralization occurs when the author wants to create an illusion of authority, or when he is using sensational language to sway the opinion of the reader. For instance, in the sentence *Everybody knows that she is a terrible teacher*, the author makes an assumption that cannot really be believed. This kind of statement is made when the author wants to create the illusion of consensus when none actually exists: it may be that most people have a negative view of the teacher, but to say that *everybody* feels that way is an exaggeration. When a reader spots overgeneralization, she should become skeptical about the argument that is being made, because an author will often try to hide a weak or unsupported assertion behind authoritative language.

Two other types of logical fallacies are **slippery slope** arguments and **hasty generalizations**. In a slippery slope argument, the author says that if something happens, it automatically means that something else will happen as a result, even though this may not be true. (i.e., just because you study hard does not mean you are going to ace the test). "Hasty generalization" is drawing a conclusion too early, without finishing analyzing the details of the argument. Writers of persuasive texts often use these techniques because they are very effective. In order to **identify logical fallacies**, readers need to read carefully and ask questions as they read. Thinking critically means not taking everything at face value. Readers need to critically evaluate an author's argument to make sure that the logic used is sound.

Organization of the Text

The way a text is organized can help the reader to understand more clearly the author's intent and his conclusions. There are various ways to organize a text, and each one has its own purposes and uses.

Some nonfiction texts are organized to **present a problem** followed by a solution. In this type of text, it is common for the problem to be explained before the solution is offered. In some cases, as when the problem is well known, the solution may be briefly introduced at the beginning. The entire passage may focus on the solution, and the problem will be referenced only occasionally. Some texts will outline multiple solutions to a problem, leaving the reader to choose among them. If the author has an interest or an allegiance to one solution, he may fail to mention or may describe inaccurately some of the other solutions. Readers should be careful of the author's agenda when reading a problem-solution text. Only by understanding the author's point of view and interests can one develop a proper judgment of the proposed solution.

Authors need to organize information logically so the reader can follow it and locate information within the text. Two common organizational structures are cause and effect and chronological order. When using **chronological order**, the author presents information in the order that it happened. For example, biographies are written in chronological order; the subject's birth and childhood are presented first, followed by their adult life, and lastly by the events leading up to the person's death.

In **cause and effect**, an author presents one thing that makes something else happen. For example, if one were to go to bed very late, they would be tired. The cause is going to bed late, with the effect of being tired the next day.

It can be tricky to identify the cause-and-effect relationships in a text, but there are a few ways to approach this task. To begin with, these relationships are often signaled with certain terms. When an author uses words like *because*, *since*, *in order*, and *so*, she is likely describing a cause-and-effect relationship. Consider the sentence, "He called her because he needed the homework." This is a simple causal relationship, in which the cause was his need for the homework and the effect was his phone call. Not all cause-and-effect relationships are marked in this way, however. Consider the sentences, "He called her. He needed the homework." When the cause-and-effect relationship is not indicated with a keyword, it can be discovered by asking why something happened. He called her: why? The answer is in the next sentence: He needed the homework.

Persuasive essays, in which an author tries to make a convincing argument and change the reader's mind, usually include cause-and-effect relationships. However, these relationships should not always be taken at face value. An author frequently will assume a cause or take an effect for granted. To read a persuasive essay effectively, one needs to judge the cause-and-effect relationships the author is presenting. For instance, imagine an author wrote the following: "The parking deck has been unprofitable because people would prefer to ride their bikes." The relationship is clear: the cause is that people prefer to ride their bikes, and the effect is that the parking deck has been unprofitable. However, a reader should consider whether this argument is conclusive. Perhaps there are other reasons for the failure of the parking deck: a down economy, excessive fees, etc. Too often, authors present causal relationships as if they are fact rather than opinion. Readers should be on the alert for these dubious claims.

Thinking critically about ideas and conclusions can seem like a daunting task. One way to make it easier is to understand the basic elements of ideas and writing techniques. Looking at the way different ideas relate to each other can be a good way for the reader to begin his analysis. For instance, sometimes writers will write about two different ideas that are in opposition to each other. The analysis of these opposing ideas is known as **contrast**. Contrast is often marred by the author's obvious partiality to one of the ideas. A discerning reader will be put off by an author who does not engage in a fair fight. In an analysis of opposing ideas, both ideas should be presented in their clearest and most reasonable terms. If the author does prefer a side, he should avoid indicating this preference with pejorative language. An analysis of opposing ideas should proceed through the major differences point by point, with a full explanation of each side's view. For instance, in an analysis of capitalism and communism, it would be important to outline each side's view on labor, markets, prices, personal responsibility, etc. It would be less effective to describe the theory of communism and then explain how capitalism has thrived in the West. An analysis of opposing views should present each side in the same manner.

Many texts follow the **compare-and-contrast** model, in which the similarities and differences between two ideas or things are explored. Analysis of the similarities between ideas is called comparison. In order for a comparison to work, the author must place the ideas or things in an equivalent structure. That is, the author must present the ideas in the same way. Imagine an author wanted to show the similarities between cricket and baseball. The correct way to do so would be to summarize the equipment and rules for each game. It would be incorrect to summarize the equipment of cricket and then lay out the history of baseball, since this would make it impossible for the reader to see the similarities. It is perhaps too obvious to say that an analysis of similar ideas should emphasize the similarities. Of course, the author should take care to include any differences that must be mentioned. Often, these small differences will only reinforce the more general similarity.

Drawing Conclusions

Authors should have a clear purpose in mind while writing. Especially when reading informational texts, it is important to understand the logical conclusion of the author's ideas. **Identifying this logical conclusion** can help the reader understand whether he agrees with the writer or not. Identifying a logical conclusion is much like making an inference: it requires the reader to combine the information given by the text with what he already knows to make a supportable assertion. If a passage is written well, then the conclusion should be obvious even when it is unstated. If the author intends the reader to draw a certain conclusion, then all of his argumentation and detail should be leading toward it. One way to approach the task of drawing conclusions is to make brief notes of all the points made by the author. When these are arranged on paper, they may clarify the logical conclusion. Another way to approach conclusions is to consider whether the reasoning of the author raises any pertinent questions. Sometimes it will be possible to draw several conclusions from a passage, and on occasion these will be conclusions that were never imagined by the author. It is essential, however, that these conclusions be supported directly by the text.

The term **text evidence** refers to information that supports a main point or points in a story, and can help lead the reader to a conclusion. Information used as *text evidence* is precise, descriptive, and factual. A main point is often followed by supporting details that provide evidence to back-up a claim. For example, a story may include the claim that winter occurs during opposite months in the Northern and Southern hemispheres. *Text evidence* based on this claim may include countries where winter occurs in opposite months, along with reasons that winter occurs at different times of the year in separate hemispheres (due to the tilt of the Earth as it rotates around the sun).

Readers interpret text and respond to it in a number of ways. Using textual support helps defend your response or interpretation because it roots your thinking in the text. You are interpreting based on information in the text and not simply your own ideas. When crafting a response, look for important quotes and details from the text to help bolster your argument. If you are writing about a character's personality trait, for example, use details from the text to show that the character acted in such a way. You can also include statistics and facts from a nonfiction text to strengthen your response. For example, instead of writing, "A lot of people use cell phones," use statistics to provide the exact number. This strengthens your argument because it is more precise.

The text used to support an argument can be the argument's downfall if it is not credible. A text is **credible**, or believable, when the author is knowledgeable and objective, or unbiased. The author's motivations for writing the text play a critical role in determining the credibility of the text and must be evaluated when assessing that credibility. The author's motives should be for the dissemination of information. The purpose of the text should be to inform or describe, not to persuade. When an author writes a persuasive text, he has the motivation that the reader will do what they want. The extent of the author's knowledge of the topic and their motivation must be evaluated when assessing the credibility of a text. Reports written about the Ozone layer by an environmental scientist and a hairdresser will have a different level of credibility.

After determining your own opinion and evaluating the credibility of your supporting text, it is sometimes necessary to communicate your ideas and findings to others. When **writing a response to a text**, it is important to use elements of the text to support your assertion or defend your position. Using supporting evidence from the text strengthens the argument because the reader can see how in depth the writer read the original piece and based their response on the details and facts within that text. Elements of text that can be used in a response include: facts, details, statistics, and direct quotations from the text. When writing a response, one must make sure they indicate which information comes from the original text and then base their discussion, argument, or defense around this information.

A reader should always be drawing conclusions from the text. Sometimes conclusions are implied from written information, and other times the information is **stated directly** within the passage. It is always more comfortable to draw conclusions from information stated within a passage, rather than to draw them from mere implications. At times an author may provide some information and then describe a counterargument. The reader should be alert for direct statements that are subsequently rejected or weakened by the author. The reader should always read the entire passage before drawing conclusions. Many readers are trained to expect the author's conclusions at either the beginning or the end of the passage, but many texts do not adhere to this format.

Drawing conclusions from information implied within a passage requires confidence on the part of the reader. **Implications** are things the author does not state directly, but which can be assumed based on what the author does say. For instance, consider the following simple passage: "I stepped outside and opened my umbrella. By the time I got to work, the cuffs of my pants were soaked." The author never states that it is raining, but this fact is clearly implied. Conclusions based on implication must be well supported by the text. In order to draw a solid conclusion, a reader should have multiple pieces of evidence, or, if he only has one, must be assured that there is no other possible explanation than his conclusion. A good reader will be able to draw many conclusions from information implied by the text, which enriches the reading experience considerably.

As an aid to drawing conclusions, the reader should be adept at **outlining** the information contained in the passage; an effective outline will reveal the structure of the passage, and will lead to solid conclusions. An effective outline will have a title that refers to the basic subject of the text, though it need not recapitulate the main idea. In most outlines, the main idea will be the first major section. It will have each major idea of the passage established as the head of a category. For instance, the most common outline format calls for the main ideas of the passage to be indicated with Roman numerals. In an effective outline of this kind, each of the main ideas will be represented by a Roman numeral and none of the Roman numerals will designate minor details or secondary ideas. Moreover, all supporting ideas and details should be placed in the appropriate place on the outline. An outline does not need to include every detail listed in the text, but it should feature all of those that are central to the argument or message. Each of these details should be listed under the appropriate main idea.

It is also helpful to **summarize** the information you have read in a paragraph or passage format. This process is similar to creating an effective outline. To begin with, a summary should accurately define the main idea of the passage, though it does not need to explain this main idea in exhaustive detail. It should continue by laying out the most important supporting details or arguments from the passage. All of the significant supporting details should be included, and none of the details included should be irrelevant or insignificant. Also, the summary should accurately report all of these details. Too often, the desire for brevity in a summary leads to the sacrifice of clarity or veracity. Summaries are often difficult to read, because they omit all of graceful language, digressions, and asides that distinguish great writing. However, if the summary is effective, it should contain much the same message as the original text.

Paraphrasing is another method the reader can use to aid in comprehension. When paraphrasing, one puts what they have read into their own words, rephrasing what the author has written to make it their own, to "translate" all of what the author says to their own words, including as many details as they can.

Test Taking Tips

Skimming

Your first task when you begin reading is to answer the question "What is the topic of the selection?" This can best be answered by quickly skimming the passage for the general idea, stopping to read only the first sentence of each paragraph. A paragraph's first sentence is usually the main topic sentence, and it gives you a summary of the content of the paragraph.

Once you've skimmed the passage, stopping to read only the first sentences, you will have a general idea about what it is about, as well as what is the expected topic in each paragraph.

Each question will contain clues as to where to find the answer in the passage. Do not just randomly search through the passage for the correct answer to each question. Search scientifically. Find key word(s) or ideas in the question that are going to either contain or be near the correct answer. These are typically nouns, verbs, numbers, or phrases in the question that will probably be duplicated in the passage. Once you have identified those key word(s) or idea, skim the passage quickly to find where those key word(s) or idea appears. The correct answer choice will be nearby.

Example: What caused Martin to suddenly return to Paris?

The key word is Paris. Skim the passage quickly to find where this word appears. The answer will be close by that word.
However, sometimes key words in the question are not repeated in the passage. In those cases, search for the general idea of the question.

Example: Which of the following was the psychological impact of the author's childhood upon the remainder of his life?

Key words are "childhood" or "psychology". While searching for those words, be alert for other words or phrases that have similar meaning, such as "emotional effect" or "mentally" which could be used in the passage, rather than the exact word "psychology".

Numbers or years can be particularly good key words to skim for, as they stand out from the rest of the text.

Example: Which of the following best describes the influence of Monet's work in the 20th century?

20th contains numbers and will easily stand out from the rest of the text. Use 20th as the key word to skim for in the passage.

Other good key word(s) may be in quotation marks. These identify a word or phrase that is copied directly from the passage. In those cases, the word(s) in quotation marks are exactly duplicated in the passage.

Example: In her college years, what was meant by Margaret's "drive for excellence"?

"Drive for excellence" is a direct quote from the passage and should be easy to find.

Once you've quickly found the correct section of the passage to find the answer, focus upon the answer choices. Sometimes a choice will repeat word for word a portion of the passage near the answer. However, beware of such duplication – it may be a trap! More than likely, the correct choice will paraphrase or summarize the related portion of the passage, rather than being exactly the same wording.

For the answers that you think are correct, read them carefully and make sure that they answer the question. An answer can be factually correct, but it MUST answer the question asked. Additionally, two answers can both be seemingly correct, so be sure to read all of the answer choices, and make sure that you get the one that BEST answers the question.

Some questions will not have a key word.

Example: Which of the following would the author of this passage likely agree with?

In these cases, look for key words in the answer choices. Then skim the passage to find where the answer choice occurs. By skimming to find where to look, you can minimize the time required.

Sometimes it may be difficult to identify a good key word in the question to skim for in the passage. In those cases, look for a key word in one of the answer choices to skim for. Often the answer choices can all be found in the same paragraph, which can quickly narrow your search.

Paragraph Focus

Focus upon the first sentence of each paragraph, which is the most important. The main topic of the paragraph is usually there.

Once you've read the first sentence in the paragraph, you have a general idea about what each paragraph will be about. As you read the questions, try to determine which paragraph will have the answer. Paragraphs have a concise topic. The answer should either obviously be there or obviously not. It will save time if you can jump straight to the paragraph, so try to remember what you learned from the first sentences.

Example: The first paragraph is about poets; the second is about poetry. If a question asks about poetry, where will the answer be? The second paragraph.

The main idea of a passage is typically spread across all or most of its paragraphs. Whereas the main idea of a paragraph may be completely different than the main idea of the very next paragraph, a main idea for a passage affects all of the paragraphs in one form or another.

Example: What is the main idea of the passage?

For each answer choice, try to see how many paragraphs are related. It can help to count how many sentences are affected by each choice, but it is best to see how many paragraphs are affected by the choice. Typically the answer choices will include incorrect choices that are main ideas of individual paragraphs, but not the entire passage. That is why it is crucial to choose ideas that are supported by the most paragraphs possible.

Eliminate Choices

Some choices can quickly be eliminated. "Andy Warhol lived there." Is Andy Warhol even mentioned in the article? If not, quickly eliminate it.

When trying to answer a question such as "the passage indicates all of the following EXCEPT" quickly skim the paragraph searching for references to each choice. If the reference exists, scratch it off as a choice. Similar choices may be crossed off simultaneously if they are close enough.

In choices that ask you to choose "which answer choice does NOT describe?" or "all of the following answer choices are identifiable characteristics, EXCEPT which?" look for answers that are similarly worded. Since only one answer can be correct, if there are two answers that appear to mean the same thing, they must BOTH be incorrect, and can be eliminated.

Example:

   a. changing values and attitudes
   b. a large population of mobile or uprooted people

These answer choices are similar; they both describe a fluid culture. Because of their similarity, they can be linked together. Since the answer can have only one choice, they can also be eliminated together.

Contextual Clues

Look for contextual clues. An answer can be right but not correct. The contextual clues will help you find the answer that is most right and is correct. Understand the context in which a phrase is stated.

When asked for the implied meaning of a statement made in the passage, immediately go find the statement and read the context it was made in. Also, look for an answer choice that has a similar phrase to the statement in question. Example: In the passage, what is implied by the phrase "Churches have become more or less part of the furniture"?

Find an answer choice that is similar or describes the phrase "part of the furniture" as that is the key phrase in the question. "Part of the furniture" is a saying that means something is fixed, immovable, or set in their ways. Those are all similar ways of saying "part of the furniture." As such, the correct answer choice will probably include a similar rewording of the expression.
Example: Why was John described as "morally desperate".

The answer will probably have some sort of definition of morals in it. "Morals" refers to a code of right and wrong behavior, so the correct answer choice will likely have words that mean something like that.

Fact/Opinion

When asked about which statement is a fact or opinion, remember that answer choices that are facts will typically have no ambiguous words. For example, how long is a long time? What defines an ordinary person? These ambiguous words of "long" and "ordinary" should not be in a factual statement. However, if all of the choices have ambiguous words, go to the context of the passage. Often a factual statement may be set out as a research finding.
Example: "The scientist found that the eye reacts quickly to change in light."

Opinions may be set out in the context of words like thought, believed, understood, or wished.

Example: "He thought the Yankees should win the World Series."

Opposites

Answer choices that are direct opposites are usually correct. The paragraph will often contain established relationships (when this goes up, that goes down). The question may ask you to draw conclusions for this and will give two similar answer choices that are opposites.

Example:

    a. a decrease in housing starts

    b. an increase in housing starts

Make Predictions

As you read and understand the passage and then the question, try to guess what the answer will be. Remember that four of the five answer choices are wrong, and once you being reading them, your mind will immediately become cluttered with answer choices designed to throw you off. Your mind is typically the most focused immediately after you have read the passage and question and digested its contents. If you can, try to predict what the correct answer will be. You may be surprised at what you can predict.

Quickly scan the choices and see if your prediction is in the listed answer choices. If it is, then you can be quite confident that you have the right answer. It still won't hurt to check the other answer choices, but most of the time, you've got it!

Answer the Question

It may seem obvious to only pick answer choices that answer the question, but the test can contain some excellent answer choices that are wrong. Don't pick an answer just because it sounds right, or you believe it to be true. It MUST answer the question. Once you've made your selection, always go back and check it against the question and make sure that you didn't misread the question, and the answer choice does answer the question posed.

Benchmark

After you read the first answer choice, decide if you think it sounds correct or not. If it doesn't, move on to the next answer choice. If it does, make a mental note about that choice. This doesn't mean that you've definitely selected it as your answer choice, it just means that it's the best you've seen thus far. Go ahead and read the next choice. If the next choice is worse than the one you've already selected, keep going to the next answer choice. If the next choice is better than the choice you've already selected, then make a mental note about that answer choice.

As you read through the list, you are mentally noting the choice you think is right. That is your new standard. Every other answer choice must be benchmarked against that standard. That choice is correct until proven otherwise by another answer choice beating it out. Once you've decided that no other answer choice seems as good, do one final check to ensure that it answers the question posed.

New Information

Correct answers will usually contain the information listed in the paragraph and question. Rarely will completely new information be inserted into a correct answer choice. Occasionally the new information may be related in a manner that the test is asking you to interpret, but seldom.

Example:

The argument above is dependent upon which of the following assumptions?

    a.   Charles's Law was used

If Charles's Law is not mentioned at all in the referenced paragraph and argument, then it is unlikely that this choice is correct. All of the information needed to answer the question is provided for you, and so you should not have to make guesses that are unsupported or choose answer choices that have unknown information that cannot be reasoned.

Valid Information

Don't discount any of the information provided in the passage, particularly shorter ones. Every piece of information may be necessary to determine the correct answer. None of the information in the paragraph is there to throw you off (while the answer choices will certainly have information to throw you off). If two seemingly unrelated topics are discussed, don't ignore either. You can be confident there is a relationship, or it wouldn't be included in the paragraph, and you are probably going to have to determine what is that relationship for the answer.

Time Management

In technical passages, do not get lost on the technical terms. Skip them and move on. You want a general understanding of what is going on, not a mastery of the passage.

When you encounter material in the selection that seems difficult to understand, it often may not be necessary and can be skipped. Only spend time trying to understand it if it is going to be relevant for a question. Understand difficult phrases only as a last resort.

Answer general questions before detail questions. A reader with a good understanding of the whole passage can often answer general questions without rereading a word. Get the easier questions out of the way before tackling the more time consuming ones.

Identify each question by type. Usually the wording of a question will tell you whether you can find the answer by referring directly to the passage or by using your reasoning powers. You alone know which question types you customarily handle with ease and which give you trouble and will require more time. Save the difficult questions for last.

Final Warnings

Word Usage Questions

When asked how a word is used in the passage, don't use your existing knowledge of the word. The question is being asked precisely because there is some strange or unusual usage of the word in the passage. Go to the passage and use contextual clues to determine the answer. Don't simply use the popular definition you already know.

Switchback Words

Stay alert for "switchbacks". These are the words and phrases frequently used to alert you to shifts in thought. The most common switchback word is "but". Others include although, however, nevertheless, on the other hand, even though, while, in spite of, despite, regardless of.

Avoid "Fact Traps"

Once you know which paragraph the answer will be in, focus on that paragraph. However, don't get distracted by a choice that is factually true about the paragraph. Your search is for the answer that answers the question, which may be about a tiny aspect in the paragraph. Stay focused and don't fall for an answer that describes the larger picture of the paragraph. Always go back to the question and make sure you're choosing an answer that actually answers the question and is not just a true statement.

Sentence Correction

Each question includes a sentence with part of it underlined. Your answer choices will offer different ways to reword or rephrase the underlined portion of the sentence. The first answer choice merely repeats the original underlined text, while the others offer different wording.

These questions will test your ability of correct and effective expression. Choose your answer carefully, utilizing the standards of written English, including grammar rules, the proper choice of words and of sentence construction. The correct answer will flow smoothly and be both clear and concise.

Use your ear

Read each sentence carefully, inserting the answer choices in the blanks. Don't stop at the first answer choice if you think it is right, but read them all. What may seem like the best choice, at first, may not be after you have had time to read all of the choices. Allow your ear to determine what sounds right. Often one or two answer choices can be immediately ruled out because it doesn't make sound logical or make sense.

Contextual clues

It bears repeating that contextual clues offer a lot of help in determining the best answer. Key words in the sentence will allow you to determine exactly which answer choice is the best replacement text.

Example:

> Archeology has shown that some of the ruins of the ancient city of Babylon are approximately 500 years <u>as old as their supposed</u> Mesopotamian predecessors.
>
> A.) as old as their supposed
>
> B.) older than their supposed

In this example, the key word "supposed" is used. Archaeology would either confirm that the predecessors to Babylon were more ancient or disprove that supposition. Since supposed was used, it would imply that archaeology had disproved the accepted belief, making Babylon actually older, not as old as, and answer choice "B" correct.

Furthermore, because "500 years" is used, answer choice A can be ruled out. Years are used to show either absolute or relative age. If two objects are as old as each other, no years are necessary to describe that relationship, and it would be sufficient to say, "The ancient city of Babylon is approximately as old as their supposed Mesopotamian predecessors," without using the term "500 years".

Simplicity is Bliss

Simplicity cannot be overstated. You should never choose a longer, more complicated, or wordier replacement if a simple one will do. When a point can be made with fewer words, choose that answer. However, never sacrifice the flow of text for simplicity. If an answer is simple, but does not make sense, then it is not correct.

Beware of added phrases that don't add anything of meaning, such as "to be" or "as to them". Often these added phrases will occur just before a colon, which may come before a list of items. However, the colon does not need a lengthy introduction. The italics phrases in the below examples are wordy and unnecessary. They should be removed and the colon placed directly after the words "sport" and "following".

Example:

There are many advantages to running as a sport, *of which the top advantages are*:

Example:

The school supplies necessary were the following, *of which a few are*:

Construction Shift

Each question starts with a sentence that you will be asked to rewrite. You will be given a short phrase with which to begin the rewritten sentence, and then asked to select the best phrase to continue, or sometimes even complete, the new sentence so that it retains the meaning of the original sentence.

Choose your answer carefully, utilizing the standards of written English, including grammar rules, the proper choice of words and of sentence construction. The correct answer will flow smoothly in a simple, clear, and concise manner.

The best strategy for tackling this part is to read the original sentence and the start of the new sentence you must create, and decide what would be the simplest way to complete the sentence, **before you look at any of the answer choices**. Once you look at the answer choices, it's easy to become confused and second guess yourself, but 90% of the time, the simplest way you can think of to rewrite the sentence will be among the choices (and will be correct).

Typically, the rewriting will involve changing a dependent clause into an independent clause, or vice versa.

Simple sentences

A simple sentence is an independent clause that contains a complete subject and a complete predicate. Simple sentences can be very short or long; the length does not indicate the complexity of the sentence. The subject may be singular or compound (more than one subject). The predicate may also be singular or compound.

Examples:

>Judy watered the lawn. (singular subject, singular predicate)
>
>Judy and Alan watered the lawn. (compound subject, Judy and Alan)
>
>Judy watered the lawn and planted flowers. (compound predicate, watered and planted)
>
>Judy and Alan watered the lawn and planted flowers. (compound subject, compound predicate)

Compound sentences

A compound sentence consists or two or more simple sentences joined together by a conjunction. Conjunctions can also be called coordinators and include: *and, but, or, nor, for, yet,* and *so.* A comma is written after the simple sentence and before the conjunction.

Example:

>I woke up at dawn, so I went outside to watch the sun rise.

A way to identify a compound sentence is to remove the conjunction and see if the two clauses can stand alone as simple sentences. In this case, *"I woke up at dawn"* and *"I went outside to watch the sunset"* can be independent; therefore it is a compound sentence.

Complex sentences

A complex sentence is comprised of an independent clause and one or more dependent clauses. The independent clause can exist alone as a sentence, while a dependent clause needs to be grouped with an independent clause, even though it has its own subject and verb.

A dependent clause, however, cannot exist alone as a sentence. Dependent clauses are linked to the independent clause with conjunctions such as *after, although, as, because, before, that, when, which,* and *while.*
Examples:

> Although he had the flu, Harry went to work.

> Marcia got married after she finished college.

Notice that the clause can appear before the independent phrase or after.

Appositives

An appositive is a noun or noun phrase that appears right after a noun to explain or rename it.
Example:

> Jane Black, the famous author, was at a book signing.

> Jim Thompson, my father, lives in Miami.

Appositives can be nonrestrictive or restrictive. Nonrestrictive appositives enhance the sentence but are not imperative to the overall meaning of the sentence. The two examples above are nonrestrictive appositives. They are set off by commas in the sentence. A restrictive appositive is essential to the sentence and does not need commas. For example: *The mailman who has black hair delivered the mail today.*

Misplaced modifiers

A modifier is a word or phrase that describes another word or phrase. A modifier should be placed next to the word(s) it is modifying to make sense. A misplaced modifier is unclear about what it is describing.

Example:

I saw the dog eating ice cream.

Was the dog eating ice cream, or did I see the dog when I was eating ice cream? The correct sentence would be: *"I saw the dog when I was eating ice cream,"* or *"When I saw the dog, I was eating ice cream."*

Modifiers—obviously—can change the meaning of sentences if used incorrectly. *"I saw the dog eating ice cream"* implies that *the dog* was eating ice cream (not me) and is thus only a good choice if that is precisely what I mean.

Parallel structure

Within a sentence, if more than one participle is given, the tense and structure must be the same.

Examples:

Sean likes boating, golfing, and to ski. (Incorrect)

Sean likes boating, golfing, and skiing. (Correct)

Sean likes to boat, to golf, and to ski. (Correct)

Sentences with incorrect parallel structure will appear awkward. Sentences with multiple clauses must have the same structure as well.

Examples:

The skaters were told that they should arrive on time and to do their stretches. (Incorrect)

The skaters were told that they should arrive on time and that they should do their stretches. (Correct)

Essay

A topic will be presented to you and you must write out a discussion on it. There is not a "correct" answer to the topic. You must evaluate the topic, organize your ideas, and develop them into a cohesive and coherent response.

You will be measured on how well you are able to utilize standard written English, organize and explain your thoughts, and support those thoughts with reasons and examples.

Brainstorm

Spend the first few minutes brainstorming out ideas. Write down any ideas you might have on the topic. The purpose is to extract from the recesses of your memory any relevant information. In this stage, anything goes down. Write down any idea, regardless of how good it may initially seem.

Strength through Diversity

The best papers will contain diversity of examples and reasoning. As you brainstorm consider different perspectives. Not only are there two sides to every issue, but there are also countless perspectives that can be considered. On any issue, different groups are impacted, with many reaching the same conclusion or position, but through vastly different paths. Try to "see" the issue through as many different eyes as you can. Look at it from every angle and from every vantage point. The more diverse the reasoning used, the more balanced the paper will become and the better the score.

Example:

The issue of free trade is not just two sided. It impacts politicians, domestic (US) manufacturers, foreign manufacturers, the US economy, the world economy, strategic alliances, retailers, wholesalers, consumers, unions, workers, and the exchange of more than just goods, but also of ideas, beliefs, and cultures. The more of these angles that you can approach the issue from, the more solid your reasoning and the stronger your position.

Furthermore, don't just use information as to how the issue impacts other people. Draw liberally from your own experience and your own observations. Explain a personal experience that you have had and your own emotions from that moment. Anything that you've seen in your community or observed in society can be expanded upon to further round out your position on the issue.

Pick a Main Idea

Once you have finished with your creative flow, stop and review it. Which idea were you able to come up with the most supporting information? It's extremely important that you pick an angle that will allow you to have a thorough and comprehensive coverage of the topic. This is not about your personal convictions, but about writing a concise rational discussion of an idea.

Weed the Garden

Every garden of ideas gets weeds in it. The ideas that you brainstormed over are going to be random pieces of information of mixed value. Go through it methodically and pick out the ones that are the best. The best ideas are strong points that it will be easy to write a few sentences or a paragraph about.

Create a Logical Flow

Now that you know which ideas you are going to use and focus upon, organize them. Put your writing points in a logical order. You have your main ideas that you will focus on, and must align them in a sequence that will flow in a smooth, sensible path from point to point, so that the reader will go smoothly from one idea to the next in a logical path. Readers must have a sense of continuity as they read your paper. You don't want to have a paper that rambles back and forth.

Start Your Engines

You have a logical flow of main ideas with which to start writing. Begin expanding on the issues in the sequence that you have set for yourself. Pace yourself. Don't spend too much time on any one of the ideas that you are expanding upon. You want to have time for all of them. Make sure you watch your time. If you have twenty minutes left to write out your ideas and you have ten ideas, then you can only use two minutes per idea. It can be a daunting task to cram a lot of information down in words in a short amount of time, but if you pace yourself, you can get through it all. If you find that you are falling behind, speed up. Move through each idea more quickly, spending less time to expand upon the idea in order to catch back up.

Once you finish expanding on each idea, go back to your brainstorming session up above, where you wrote out your ideas. Go ahead and erase the ideas as you write about them. This will let you see what you need to write about next, and also allow you to pace yourself and see what you have left to cover.

First Paragraph

Your first paragraph should have several easily identifiable features.

First, it should have a quick description or paraphrasing of the topic. Use your own words to briefly explain what the topic is about.

Second, you should explain your opinion of the topic and give an explanation of why you feel that way. What is your decision or conclusion on the topic?

Third, you should list your "writing points". What are the main ideas that you came up with earlier? This is your opportunity to outline the rest of your paper. Have a sentence explaining each idea that you will go intend further depth in additional paragraphs. If someone was to only read this paragraph, they should be able to get an "executive summary" of the entire paper.

Body Paragraph

Each of your successive paragraphs should expand upon one of the points listed in the main paragraph. Use your personal experience and knowledge to support each of your points. Examples should back up everything.

Conclusion Paragraph

Once you have finished expanding upon each of your main points, wrap it up. Summarize what you have said and covered in a conclusion paragraph. Explain once more your opinion of the topic and quickly review why you feel that way. At this stage, you have already backed up your statements, so there is no need to do that again. All you are doing is refreshing in the mind of the reader the main points that you have made.

Don't Panic

Panicking will not put down any more words on paper for you. Therefore, it isn't helpful. When you first see the topic, if your mind goes as blank as the page on which you have to write out your paper, take a deep breath. Force yourself to mechanically go through the steps listed above.

Secondly, don't get clock fever. It's easy to be overwhelmed when you're looking at a page that doesn't seem to have much text, there is a lot of blank space further down, your mind is full of random thoughts and feeling confused, and the clock is ticking down faster than you would like. You brainstormed first so that you don't have to keep coming up with ideas. If you're running out of time and you have a lot of ideas that you haven't expanded upon, don't be afraid to make some cuts. Start picking the best ideas that you have left and expand on those few. Don't feel like you have to write down and expand all of your ideas.

Check Your Work

It is more important to have a shorter paper that is well written and well organized, than a longer paper that is poorly written and poorly organized. Don't keep writing about a subject just to add words and sentences, and certainly don't start repeating yourself. Expand on the ideas that you identified in the brainstorming session and make sure that you save yourself a few minutes at the end to go back and check your work.

Leave time at the end, at least a few minutes, to go back and check over your work. Reread and make sure that everything you've written makes sense and flows. Clean up any spelling or grammar mistakes that you might have made. Also, go ahead and erase any brainstorming ideas that you weren't able to expand upon and clean up any other extraneous information that you might have written that doesn't fit into your paper.

As you proofread, make sure there aren't any fragments or run-ons. Check for sentences that are too short or too long. If the sentence is too short, look to see if you have an identifiable subject and verb. If it is too long, break it up into two separate sentences. Watch out for any "big" words you may have used. It's good to use difficult vocabulary words, but only if you are positive that you are using them correctly. Your paper has to be correct, it doesn't have to be fancy. You're not trying to impress anyone with your vocabulary, just your ability to develop and express ideas.

Final Note

Depending on your test taking preferences and personality, the essay writing will probably be your hardest or your easiest section. You are required to go through the entire process of writing a paper very quickly, which can be quite a challenge.

Focus upon each of the steps listed above. Go through the process of creative flow first, generating ideas and thoughts about the topic. Then organize those ideas into a smooth logical flow. Pick out the ones that are best from the list you have created. Decide which main idea or angle of the topic you will discuss.

Create a recognizable structure in your paper, with an introductory paragraph explaining what you have decided upon, and what your main points will be. Use the body paragraphs to expand on those main points and have a conclusion that wraps up the issue or topic.

Save a few moments to go back and review what you have written. Clean up any minor mistakes that you might have had and give it those last few critical touches that can make a huge difference. Finally, be proud and confident of what you have written!

Practice Test

Sentence Skills

Sentence Correction

Directions for questions 1–10
Select the best version of the underlined part of the sentence. The first choice is the same as the original sentence. If you think the original sentence is best, choose the first answer.

1. Several theories <u>about what caused dinosaurs to have extinction exist,</u> but scientists are still unable to reach a concrete conclusion.
    A. about what caused dinosaurs to have extinction exist
    B. about what caused dinosaurs to become extinct exist
    C. about the causes of the dinosaur extinction exists
    D. regarding the cause of extinction of dinosaurs exist

2. <u>Although most persons</u> prefer traditional pets like cats and dogs, others gravitate towards exotic animals like snakes and lizards.
    A. Although most persons
    B. Because most people
    C. While most people
    D. Maybe some persons

3. It is important that software companies offer tech support <u>to customers who are encountering problems</u>.
    A. to customers who are encountering problems
    B. because not all customers encounter problems
    C. with customers who encounter problems
    D. to customer who is encountering difficulties

4. The fact <u>that children eat high fat diets and watch excessive amount of television are a cause of concern</u> for many parents.
    A. that children eat high fat diets and watch excessive amount of television are a cause of concern
    B. the children eat high fat diets and watches excessive amount of television are a cause of concern
    C. is children eat high fat diets and watch excessive amount of television is a cause for concern
    D. that children eat high fat diets and watch excessive amounts of television is a cause for concern

- 92 -

5. <u>Contrarily to popular beliefs</u>, bats do not actually entangle themselves in the hair of humans on purpose.
    A. Contrarily to popular beliefs
    B. Contrary to popular belief
    C. Contrary to popularity belief
    D. Contrary to popular believing

6. <u>Considering how long ago the Ancient Egyptians lived, it's amazing</u> we know anything about them at all.
    A. Considering how long ago the Ancient Egyptians lived, it's amazing
    B. Consider how long the Ancient Egyptians lived, it's amazing
    C. Considering for how long the Ancient Egyptians lived, its amazing
    D. Considering, how long ago the Ancient Egyptians lived, its amazing

7. <u>Because technology has constantly changed</u>, those employed in the IT industry must learn new skills continuously.
    A. Because technology has constantly changed
    B. Because technology is constantly changing
    C. Even though technology is changing
    D. Despite the fact that technology has changed

8. <u>To mix, shade, and highlighting</u> are essential skills that every beginning artist must master.
    A. To mix, shade, and highlighting
    B. Mix, shade, and highlighting
    C. To mixing, shading, and highlighting
    D. Mixing, shading, and highlighting

9. The growing problem of resistance to antibiotics can be attributed, in part, <u>to the fact that they are prescribed unnecessarily</u>.
    A. to the fact that they are prescribed unnecessarily
    B. in the facts that they are prescribed unnecessarily
    C. to the fact that they are prescribing unnecessarily
    D. with the facts that they are being prescribed unnecessarily.

10. <u>A key challenges facing university graduates</u> searching for employment is that most have limited work experience.
    A. A key challenges facing university graduates
    B. Key challenge faced by university graduates
    C. A key challenge facing university graduates
    D. Key challenges facing university's graduates

Construction Shift

Directions for questions 11–20
Rewrite the sentence in your head following the directions given below. Keep in mind that your new sentence should be well written and should have essentially the same meaning as the original sentence.

11. Mitosis is the process of cell division, and if there are errors during this process, it can result in serious complications.

Rewrite, beginning with

Serious complications can result

The next words will be
    A. during the process of cell division
    B. if there are errors during the process
    C. in the process of mitosis
    D. when this process leads to errors

12. It was a very tough decision, but Sharon finally decided after much consideration to study biology at Yale University.

Rewrite, beginning with

After much consideration
The next words will be
    A. Sharon finally decided to study
    B. it was a very tough decision
    C. Sharon studied biology at Yale University
    D. a very tough study was decided.

13. Small business owners must compete with larger stores by providing excellent service, because department store prices are simply too low for owners of small businesses to match them.

Rewrite, beginning with

Prices in department stores are simply too low for owners of small businesses to match them,
The next words will be
    A. so small business owners must
    B. while small business owners must
    C. when small business owners must
    D. because small business owners must

14. Ants are fascinating creatures, and some of their unique characteristics are their strength, organizational skills, and construction talents.

Rewrite, beginning with

Strength, organizational skills, and construction talents
The next words will be
    A. are some of the unique characteristics
    B. are possessed by fascinating creatures
    C. of ants are fascinating characteristics
    D. are unique characteristics of their

15. Many people do not regularly wear their seatbelts, even though law enforcement professionals warn motorists about the dangers of not doing so.

Rewrite, beginning with

Despite warnings by law enforcement professionals
The next words will be
    A. motorists ignore the dangers of not doing so
    B. many people do not regularly wear their seatbelts
    C. about the people who don't wear seatbelts
    D. even though motorists do not wear seatbelts

16. The wolverine is an incredibly strong animal that is actually closely related to weasels, and not, as many people believe, related to wolves.

Rewrite, beginning with

Many people believe the wolverine is
The next words will be
    A. closely related to weasels
    B. an incredibly strong animal
    C. related to wolves
    D. a weasel, but they are actually

17. Advertising aimed at children is of greater concern than that aimed towards adults because children are more likely to internalize the messages presented in print and television ads.

Rewrite, beginning with

<u>Because children are more likely to internalize the messages presented in ads,</u>
The next words will be
    A. advertising aimed at children
    B. advertising aimed towards adults
    C. is of greater concern than that
    D. print and television advertisements

18. Increasing housing and fuel costs in the United States have caused many people to accumulate high levels of consumer and credit debt, and this is particularly true for people who have limited incomes.

Rewrite, beginning with

<u>Many people have accumulated high levels of debt</u>
The next words will be
    A. for those who have limited income
    B. mainly in the United States
    C. due to increasing housing and fuel costs
    D. for consumer and credit

19. People and companies who sell products online often charge a lot for shipping, which is why even though it is possible to find low prices online, customers may not be saving as much money as they think.

Rewrite, beginning with

<u>Customers may not be saving as much money as they think</u>
The next words will be
    A. which is why it is possible to charge for shipping
    B. because people and companies who sell
    C. because it is possible to find low prices
    D. when people and companies shop online

20. In the world of stock option trading, purchasing a put gives an individual the right to sell shares, so they will likely profit if the value of a company's stock decreases, but not if it increases.

Rewrite, beginning with

<u>An individual will profit if the value of a company's stock decreases</u>
The next words will be
    A. in the world of stock option trading
    B. giving them a right to sell shares
    C. or if it increases
    D. if he purchases a put

Reading Comprehension

Directions for questions 1–10
Read the statement or passage and then choose the best answer to the question. Answer the question based on what is stated or implied in the statement or passage.

1. During the 1970s, a new type of pet became popular in North America. Although they were actually just brine shrimp, they were marketed as "Sea Monkeys." They don't actually look like monkeys at all, but were branded as such due to their long tails. When sea monkeys first began to be sold in the United States, they were sold under the brand name "Instant Life." Later, when they became known as sea monkeys, the cartoon drawings that were featured in comic books showed creatures that resembled humans more than shrimp. The creative marketing of these creatures can only be described as genius, and at the height of their popularity in the 1970s, they could be found in as many as one in five homes.

Based on the information in the passage, it can be inferred that
    A. Sea monkeys were more popular when they were marketed as "instant life."
    B. Sea monkeys wouldn't have been as popular if they had been marketed as "brine shrimp."
    C. Most people thought they were actually purchasing monkeys that lived in the sea.
    D. There are more homes today that have sea monkeys than there were in the 1970s.

2. Before the battle between CDs and MP3s, there was a rivalry during the 1960s between the four-track and the eight-track tape. Four-track tapes were invented in the early 1960s by Earl Muntz, an entrepreneur from CaliforniA. Later, Bill Lear designed the eight-track tape. This latter invention was similar in size to the four-track tape, but it could store and play twice as many songs. Lear had close ties with the motor company Ford, and he convinced them to include eight-track players in their vehicles, which definitely helped the eight-track tape to achieve a high level of popularity. Soon after, they began being used in homes, and the four-track tape all but disappeared.

The main difference between the four-track and eight-track tape was
   A. The four-track tape was much larger than the eight-track tape.
   B. The eight-track tape cost a lot more to produce than the four-track tape.
   C. The eight-track tape could hold more songs than the four-track tape.
   D. The four-track tape was usually included in Ford vehicles.

3. It is natural for humans to have fears, but when those fears are completely irrational and begin to interfere with everyday activities they are known as phobias. Agoraphobia is a serious phobia, and it can be devastating for those who suffer from it. Contrary to popular belief, agoraphobia is not simply a fear of open spaces. Rather, the agoraphobic fears being in a place that he feels is unsafe. Depending on the severity of the problem, the agoraphobic might fear going to the mall, walking down the street, or even walking to the mailbox. Often, the agoraphobic will view his home as the safest possible place to be, and he may even be reluctant to leave his house. Treatments for this condition include medication and behavioral therapy.

An agoraphobic would feel safest
   A. In their yard.
   B. In their house.
   C. In a mall.
   D. On the sidewalk.

4. The butterfly effect is a somewhat poorly understood mathematical concept, primarily because it is interpreted and presented incorrectly by the popular mediA.   It refers to systems, and how initial conditions can influence the ultimate outcome of an event. The best way to understand the concept is through an example. You have two rubber balls. There are two inches between them, and you release them. Where will they end up? Well, that depends. If they're in a sloped, sealed container, they will end up two inches away from each other at the end of the slope. If it's the top of a mountain, however, they may end up miles away from each other. They could bounce off rocks; one could get stuck in a snow bank while the other continues down the slope; one could enter a river and get swept away. The fact that even a tiny initial difference can have a significant overall impact is known as the butterfly effect.

The purpose of this passage is
   A. To discuss what could happen to two rubber balls released on top of a mountain.
   B. To show why you can predict what will happen to two objects in a sloped, sealed container.
   C. To discuss the primary reason why the butterfly effect is a poorly understood concept.
   D. To give an example of how small changes at the beginning of an event can have large effects.

5. Wells provide water for drinking, bathing, and cleaning to many people across the world. When wells are being dug, there are several issues that must be taken into account to minimize the chance of potential problems down the road. First, it's important to be aware that groundwater levels differ, depending on the season. In general, groundwater levels will be higher during the winter. So if a well is being dug during the winter, it should be deep enough to remain functional during the summer, when water levels are lower. Well water that is used is replaced by melting snow and rain. If the well owners are using the water faster than it can be replaced, however, the water levels will be lowered. The only way to remedy this, aside from waiting for the groundwater to be replenished naturally, is to deepen the well.

From this passage, it can be concluded that
   A. It is better to have a well that is too deep than one that is too shallow.
   B. Most well owners will face significant water shortages every year.
   C. Most people who dig wells during the winter do not make them deep enough.
   D. Well water is safe to use for bathing and cleaning, but is not suitable for drinking.

6. Today's low-fat craze has led many people to assume that all fats are unhealthy, but this is simply not the case. Fat is an essential component of any healthy diet because it provides energy and helps the body process nutrients. While all fats should be consumed in moderation, there are good and bad fats. Good fats are what are known as unsaturated fats. They are found in olive oil, fatty fish like salmon, and nuts. Bad fats are saturated and trans fats. They are found in foods like butter, bacon, and ice cream. Consumption of foods that contain trans or saturated fats should be restricted or avoided altogether.

The main purpose of this passage is to
    A. Explain why fat is important for the body.
    B. Discuss some of the main sources of good fats.
    C. Talk about the different types of fats.
    D. Discuss examples of foods that should be avoided.

7. Satire is a genre that originated in the ancient world and is still popular today. Although satire is often humorous, its purposes and intentions go well beyond simply making people laugh. Satire is a way for the playwright, author, or television producer to criticize society, human nature, and individuals that he holds in contempt. Satire as we know it today developed in Ancient Greece and Rome. There were three main types. The first, Menippean satire, focused on criticizing aspects of human nature. This was done by introducing stereotypical, one-dimensional characters. Horatian satire can be viewed as gentle satire. It made fun of people and their habits, but in a way that was not offensive. Juvenalian satire was written is such a way that the audience would experience feelings of disgust and aversion when they saw the characters and their actions. Some of the most popular satires today are fake news shows, like the *Daily Show* and the *Colbert Report*, and satirical comic strips like *Doonesbury*.

The main purpose of the passage is
    A. To discuss the history of satire.
    B. To present the major types of satire.
    C. To discuss modern examples of satire.
    D. To present the purposes of satire.

8. Many people believe that how we express our feelings is mainly determined by our upbringing and culture. Undoubtedly, this is true in some cases. In North America, for example, it is customary to shake hands when we meet somebody to express acceptance, whereas in other countries they may simply bow slightly to indicate this. Many feelings, however, are expressed in similar ways by people all over the world. These emotions include, fear, anger, happiness, disgust, and sorrow. For example, if a person is experiencing fear, their eyes will widen and their pupils will dilate. This reaction is largely involuntary. The finding that people express many feelings in a similar manner, regardless of where they are from, indicates that facial expressions are influenced more by evolution than culture.

Based on the passage, it can be concluded that
   A. People often can't hide what they are feeling.
   B. People from other parts of the world express happiness differently.
   C. Fear is the only emotion that is felt by everybody in the worlD.
   D. Acceptance is a feeling invented by man.

9. Cities are typically warmer than the surrounding countryside, a phenomenon known as the heat island effect. There are numerous causes of this phenomenon, including emissions from cars and buildings. This creates a mini greenhouse effect. In rural areas, the standing water in marshes and ponds evaporates, which cools the air slightly. This does not occur to the same extent in the city. The tall buildings in the center of most cities block winds that would provide some relief from the excessive heat. Finally, the color and material of most roads and buildings absorbs rather than reflects heat. Although planting trees and using building materials that reflect heat may alleviate the problem somewhat, it will by no means eliminate it.

The main purpose of the passage is to
   A. Talk about how the problem of heat island can be solved.
   B. Argue that cities should make an effort to plant more trees.
   C. Present the major causes of the problem of heat island.
   D. Contrast the city environment to that of the countryside.

10. Marsupials resemble mammals in a number of ways. For one thing, they are warm-blooded creatures. They have hair, and the mothers feed their young by producing milk. However, one thing that separates marsupials from mammals is that their young are born when they are not yet fully-developed. Most are born after only about four or five weeks. They finish their development in the pouch of their mother. Some of the more commonly known marsupials are koalas, kangaroos, and opossums. They are a diverse group, with many members having little in common besides their reproductive traits.

A major difference between marsupials and mammals is
   A. Marsupials have hair, while mammals do not.
   B. Mammals are a much more diverse group than marsupials.
   C. Marsupials are born at an earlier stage of development.
   D. Mammals feed their young by producing milk.

Directions for questions 11–20
For the questions that follow, two underlined sentences are followed by a question or statement. Read the sentences, then choose the best answer to the question or the best completion of the statement.

11. Atheists are individuals who do not believe in any type of higher power. Theists usually possess religious and spiritual beliefs and have faith in one or more gods.

What does the second sentence do?
   A. It states an example.
   B. It makes a contrast.
   C. It disputes the first sentence.
   D. It offers a solution.

12. Home schooling refers to the practice of educating children at home rather than sending them to school. Home schooling usually involves one parent giving up their career in order to stay home.

What does the second sentence do?
   A. It restates the information from the first.
   B. It provides an example.
   C. It states an effect.
   D. It contradicts the first.

13. Coffee is the most popular beverage in the entire world, and it is estimated that about 80% of Americans drink coffee.
According to a recent study, about 85% of North Americans drink soda, making it the most popular drink worldwide.

What does the second sentence do?
    A. It makes a contrast.
    B. It gives an example.
    C. It supports the first.
    D. It contradicts the first.

14. Regeneration refers to the ability that some animals have to replace severed body parts.
A salamander that has had its tail chopped off can grow a new one that is practically identical to the original.

What does the second sentence do?
    A. It restates the information from the first.
    B. It provides an example.
    C. It supports the first.
    D. It presents a solution.

15. Even though monthly rent on an apartment is usually less than a mortgage payment, most people would still rather own their own home.
Home ownership is a dream for most North Americans, even though monthly costs for houses are higher than those for apartments.

What does the second sentence do?
    A. It contradicts the first.
    B. It supports the first.
    C. It restates the information in the first.
    D. It explains the information in the first.

16. Soil contamination can be caused by a wide variety of factors, including leakage from underground septic tanks.
Septic tanks will corrode over time, and when they leak or rupture, the contents contaminate the surrounding soil.

What does the second sentence do?
    A. It expands on the first.
    B. It restates the information in the first.
    C. It states an effect.
    D. It proposes a solution.

17. The Richter Scale is the most commonly-used method to measure the strength of earthquakes.
Even though other methods are used more frequently to measure earthquakes, the Richter Scale is the most trusted.

What does the second sentence do?
   A. It provides an example.
   B. It reinforces the information in the first.
   C. It contradicts the information in the first.
   D. It presents a conclusion.

18. Adaptation refers to the ability of an animal to change in order to be better suited for its environment and to increase its chances of survival.
Porcupines have sharp quills that can be used to ward off animals that might otherwise try to hunt them.

What does the second sentence do?
   A. It expands on the information in the first.
   B. It presents an example.
   C. It states an effect.
   D. It makes an inference.

19. Congestion due to excessive traffic means that many people are forced to sit in traffic on their way to work.
Carpooling and public transportation can effectively reduce the number of cars on the road.

How are the two sentences related?
   A. They explain several concepts.
   B. They provide a concept and an example.
   C. They support one another.
   D. They state a problem and a solution.

20. Men are known for being analytical when they make decisions.
Women often make decisions based on intuition and gut feelings.

What does the second sentence do?
   A. It gives an example.
   B. It expands on the first.
   C. It provides a contrast.
   D. It contradicts the first.

Arithmetic Test

Solve the following problems and select your answer from the choices given. You may use the paper you have been given for scratch paper.

1. 6/12 is equivalent to which fraction?
   A. 10/24
   B. 3/4
   C. 3/6
   D. 1/6

2. $675 \times 7 =$
   A. 4,535
   B. 4,675
   C. 4,865
   D. 4,725

3. Which of the following is closest to 5,465 + 394?
   A. 5,000
   B. 5,500
   C. 6,000
   D. 6,500

4. $11/12 - 1/6 =$
   A. 1/4
   B. 1/2
   C. 3/4
   D. 5/6

5. $743 - 87 =$
   A. 626
   B. 656
   C. 674
   D. 694

6. $75 \div 16 =$
   A. 4.69
   B. 5.23
   C. 6.05
   D. 7.39

7. $598 \times 46 =$
   A. 26,014
   B. 26,182
   C. 27,295
   D. 27,508

8. Which of the following is closest to 0.35?
   A. 1/4
   B. 1/3
   C. 1/2
   D. 3/5

9. 6.52 + 0.2 + 0.05 =
   A. 6.57
   B. 6.75
   C. 6.77
   D. 6.95

10. 9/5 =
   A. 0.56
   B. 0.95
   C. 1.5
   D. 1.8

11. 0.058 / 6.37 =
   A. 0.005
   B. 0.009
   C. 0.04
   D. 0.08

12. Which of the following represents the largest value?
   A. 0.0095
   B. 0.008
   C. 0.072
   D. 0.069

13. Kate got a 56 on her first math test. On her second math test, she raised her grade by 12%. What was her grade?
   A. 62.7
   B. 67.2
   C. 68.0
   D. 72.3

14. A factory can produce 12 tonnes of cereal per day. A customer has ordered 596 tonnes of cereal. How many days will it take the factory to fill the customer's order?
   A. 48
   B. 50
   C. 52
   D. 54

15. If one side of a square has a length of 56 cm, what is its perimeter?
    A. 112 cm
    B. 224 cm
    C. 448 cm
    D. 3136 cm

16. Four people decide to adopt a dog and take turns caring for it. Person A thinks he can take care of the dog 1/4 of the time; person B thinks she can handle 1/8; person C thinks he can take care of the dog 1/2 of the time. What part of the fourth person's time will have to be spent caring for the dog?
    A. 1/8
    B. 1/4
    C. 1/3
    D. 1/2

17. A skyscraper is 548 meters high. The building's owners decide to increase its height by 3%. How high would the skyscraper be after the increase?
    A. 551 meters
    B. 555 meters
    C. 562 meters
    D. 564 meters

Elementary Algebra

Solve the following problems and select your answer from the choices given. You may use the paper you have been given for scratch paper.

1. $5(80 / 8) + (7 - 2) - (9 \times 5) =$
   A. -150
   B. 10
   C. 100
   D. 230

2. $-32(-9) + 7 =$
   A. −281
   B. −64
   C. 34
   D. 295

3. $275 - (-64) - 32 =$
   A. 179
   B. 243
   C. 307
   D. 371

4. If $|x \cdot 3| = 2$, what does x equal?
   A. 2/3
   B. 6
   C. -2/3 or 2/3
   D. -6 or 6

5. $9x - 3y + 8xy - 3$
   If $x = 10$ and $y = -2$, what is the value of this expression?
   A. -67
   B. -61
   C. -79
   D. 241

6. Simplify the following: $9x(3x^2 + 2x - 9)$
   A. $27x^2 + 18x - 81$
   B. $27x^3 + 18x^2 - 81x$
   C. $12x^3 + 11x^2 - x$
   D. $27x^3 + 18x^2 - 18x$

7. Evaluate the following expression, if $x = 3$.
   $x^5x^2 + y^0 =$
   A. 59,049
   B. 59,050
   C. 2,187
   D. 2,188

8. Expand the following expression: $(2x - 5)(x + 7)$
   A. $2x^2 + 9x - 35$
   B. $11x - 35$
   C. $2x^2 - 19x - 35$
   D. $2x^2 + 9x + 35$

9. If x represents the number of students that paid \$100 for a new textbook and y represents the number of students that paid \$50 for a used textbook, which of the following represents the total amount that was spent on used textbooks?
   A. $150y$
   B. $100x$
   C. $50y$
   D. $50x$

10. In the following inequality, solve for x.

$-4x + 8 \geq 48$

   A. $x \geq 10$
   B. $x \geq -10$
   C. $x \leq 10$
   D. $x \leq -10$

11. $x^2 + 12x + 36 = 0$
What is the value of x?

   A. $x = 6$
   B. $x = -6$
   C. $x = 6, -6$
   D. $x = 0, 6$

12. $56x + 23 = -14$
What is the value of x?

   A. -0.66
   B. 0.66
   C. 0.16
   D. -0.16

College Level Math Test

Solve the following problems and select your answer from the choices given. You may use the paper you have been given for scratch paper.

1. Simplify the following expression.

$$\frac{64x^4 + 8x^3 - 4x^2 + 16x}{8x}$$

   A. $56x^3 - 12x^2 + 8$
   B. $8x^3 + x^2 - 1/2x + 2$
   C. $8x^4 + x^3 - 1/2x^2 + 2x$
   D. $8x^3 + x^2 - 2x + 2$

2. Factor the following expression.
$9x^2y - 18xy - 27y$

   A. $9(x^2y - 2xy - 3y)$
   B. $9y(x + 3)(x + 1)$
   C. $9y(x - 3)(x+1)$
   D. $9y(x + 3)(x - 1)$

3. Simplify the following expression.

$\sqrt{3}(5\sqrt{3} - \sqrt{12} + \sqrt{10})$

A. $9 + \sqrt{30}$

B. $15 - \sqrt{15} + \sqrt{13}$

C. $15\sqrt{3} - 3\sqrt{12} + 3\sqrt{10}$

D. $3 - \sqrt{13}$

4. $25x - 12x + 6x - 27 = 35$

Solve for x.

A. $x = 0.42$

B. $x = 1.44$

C. $x = 3.26$

D. $x = 5.23$

5. $(y + 10)^2 - 625 = 0$

Solve for y.

A. $y = 615$

B. $y = -15, 15$

C. $y = -15$

D. $y = 15, -35$

6. Solve for y using the following system of equations.

$2x - 6y = 12$

$-6x + 14y = 42$

A. -19.5

B. -52.5

C. -2.44

D. 6.56

7. If $6x + 2x - 26 = -5x$, then $[(2x-1)/7]^3 =$

A. 0.08

B. 0.19

C. 1.29

D. 12.7

8. A line passes through points A (-3, 18) and B (5, 2). What is the slope of the line?

A. 2

B. -2

C. 1/2

D. -1/2

9. Which of the following lines is perpendicular to the line $y = -5x + 27$?

A. $y = 5x + 27$

B. $y = -1/5x + 27$

C. $y = 1/5x + 27$

D. $y = 1/5x - 27$

10. What is the midpoint of points A (-20, 8) and B (5, 3)?
    A. (5.5, 7.5)
    B. (7.5, 5.5)
    C. (5.5, -7.5)
    D. (-7.5, 5.5)

11. If $f(x) = 4x - 32$, what is the value of $f(x$-$5)$?
    A. $f(x - 5) = 4x$ - 52
    B. $f(x - 5) = 13$
    C. $f(x - 5) = 4x$ - 1
    D. $f(x - 5) = 3$

12. Given that $f(x) = 8x + 64$, find the value of $f^{-1}(x)$.
    A. $f^{-1}(x) = $-$8x$ - 64
    B. $f^{-1}(x) = 1/8x$ - 8
    C. $f^{-1}(x) = $-$1/8x$ -8
    D. $f^{-1}(x) = x - 8$

13. What is the range of the following function?
    $y = 3x^2 + 16x + 5$
    A. $y \leq 3$
    B. $y \geq 16$
    C. $y \leq 0$
    D. $y \geq 5$

14. If $f(x) = 9^x 8^x + 6x - 12$, then $f(3) = $
    A. 373,254
    B. 373, 452
    C. 1,247
    D. 654

15. What is the range of the function $y = 3\sin 2x$?
    A. All real numbers
    B. All numbers between -3 and +3
    C. All numbers between -2 and +2
    D. All positive integers

16. In a right triangle, one side is 6cm and another is 8cm. What is the length of the hypotenuse?
    A. 3.5cm
    B. 100cm
    C. 10cm
    D. 196cm

17. Simply the following: $\dfrac{5}{6i}$

    A. $-\dfrac{5}{6}i$

    B. $\dfrac{5}{6}i$

    C. $\sqrt{5}/6\,i$

    D. $\dfrac{25}{6}i$

18. If A = $\begin{matrix} 9 & 6 & 5 \\ 7 & 4 & 6 \\ 1 & 1 & 1 \end{matrix}$ and B = $\begin{matrix} 5 & 2 & 9 \\ 7 & 4 & 1 \\ 8 & 6 & 8 \end{matrix}$ what is the value of A + B?

    A. $\begin{matrix} 15 & 8 & 14 \\ 14 & 8 & 7 \\ 9 & 7 & 9 \end{matrix}$

    B. $\begin{matrix} 14 & 8 & 14 \\ 14 & 8 & 7 \\ 9 & 7 & 9 \end{matrix}$

    C. $\begin{matrix} 14 & 9 & 14 \\ 14 & 8 & 7 \\ 9 & 7 & 9 \end{matrix}$

    D. $\begin{matrix} 14 & 8 & 14 \\ 14 & 8 & 7 \\ 8 & 8 & 8 \end{matrix}$

19. A child is given a set of 6 different colored blocks. How many different combinations will he be able to make with these blocks?

    A. 6

    B. 36

    C. 720

    D. 46,656

20. Use factorials to express the following: $^{15}P_9$

    A. $\dfrac{15!}{9!}$

    B. P(15/9)

    C. (15/9)!

    D. $\dfrac{15!}{6!}$

Written Essay

Prepare an essay of about 300-600 words on the topic below.

Some people believe that everybody should vote in every election. They say that voting is an important democratic right that everybody should exercise whenever possible. Other people think that voting is not that important. They feel that if none of the candidates are offering anything that will benefit them, they are making a strong statement by not voting. Write an essay to someone who is deciding whether or not they should vote in the next election and take a position on whether you believe they should vote even if none of the candidates appeal to them. Use examples and arguments to support your position.

Answer Explanations

Sentence Skills

Sentence Correction

1. B: The phrase *to have extinction* in choice A is grammatically incorrect. In choice C, *causes* is plural, and so the word should be *exist* rather than *exists*. D is not the best choice because it is somewhat awkward. B sounds the best and is also grammatically correct.

2. C: C is the best answer because it indicates a contrast and is grammatically correct.

3. A: A is the best answer because it denotes the party to whom companies are offering tech support and because the verb *are* agrees with the noun *customers*.

4. D: D is the best choice. The phrases *high-fat diets* and *excessive amounts of television* agree with each other because they are both plural. The word *is* refers to *the fact that*, so these also agree with each other.

5. B: This is a well-known phrase meaning *despite what most people believe*. The word *contrarily* in choice A makes it incorrect. *Popularity* in choice C is out of place, and *believing* in choice D is incorrect.

6. A: B implies the Egyptians had long life spans, which doesn't make sense in the context of the sentence. C uses *its* instead of the grammatically correct *it's*, while D has misplaced commas and also uses *its*. A indicates the Egyptians lived a long time ago, and the correct form of *it's* is used.

7. B: The sentence describes a cause/effect relationship, so *because* is the correct way to begin the sentence. Choice A implies that technology changed in the past, which does not make sense in the context of the sentence. B indicates a cause/effect relationship, and states that technology is continuously changing, which is why IT professionals must continuously learn new skills.

8. D: D is the correct choice because the three verbs are in the same form. A and B use different verb forms. C is grammatically incorrect because of the *to* that is used to begin the sentence.

9. A: Saying that something can be *attributed to* something else is grammatically correct, which eliminates choices B and D. C is incorrect because *they* refers to antibiotics, so the sentence is essentially stating that antibiotics are prescribing.

Inanimate objects are incapable of doing this, which makes the sentence incorrect. A states that antibiotics are prescribed, indicating someone else is doing the prescribing, which makes it the correct choice.

10. C: A is incorrect because *a* and *challenges* do not agree. B is incorrect because *key challenge* must be prefaced by *A* D is incorrect because of the misplaced apostrophe, and also because the sentence only identifies one challenge, meaning the plural, *key challenges*, is incorrect.

Construction Shift

11. B: The original sentence states that serious complications can result if there are errors during the process of cell division. A and C refer to the process of cell division only, and not the errors that must be made for complications to occur. D indicates that the process leads to errors, rather than that the errors occur during the process.

12. A: The original sentence states that after much consideration a decision was made, which is why A is the best choice. The decision wasn't still difficult after much consideration, as B indicates, and she didn't immediately attend university, as is indicated by C. D simply doesn't make sense in the context of the statement.

13. A: A is the best choice because it is the only one that indicates a cause/effect relationship. Small business owners must do something *because* prices in department stores are too low for small business owners to match them.

14. A: The rewritten sentence begins with examples of some of the unique characteristics of ants. B does not indicate that they are unique characteristics; C describes them as fascinating rather than unique; and D does not make sense in the context of the sentence because of the phrase *of their* that follows *are unique characteristics*.

15. B: The word *despite* indicates that something is done in spite of warnings by law enforcement professionals, which eliminates choices C and D. A does not indicate precisely what motorists are failing to do, which eliminates that choice. B is the correct answer.

16. C: The original sentence states that many people believe the wolverine is related to wolves. They are related to weasels, but this is not something many people believe, eliminating choices A and C. The original sentence describes the strength of wolverines as a fact rather than a belief, eliminating choice B.

17. A: The word *because* indicates a cause/effect relationship. Since the phrase focuses on children, choice B can be eliminated. C does not indicate what "is of greater concern," so it can be eliminated. D is basically just describing the different types of ads, essentially restating something that has already been said. Answer

choice A focuses on children and identifies advertising as the focus of the sentence, making it the best choice.

18. C: C is the only choice that offers an explanation as to why people have accumulated debt. A and D cannot logically follow the introductory phrase. B was not a fact expressed in the original sentence.

19. B: A indicates shipping costs can be charged because consumers are not saving as much money as they think, which is not an idea expressed in the original sentence. C states they may not be saving as much money as they think because they can find low prices, an idea that is also not stated in the original sentence. D indicates that companies shop online, an idea not expressed in the original sentence. B indicates there is a reason why people are not saving as much as they think. It then identifies people and companies, which are also identified in the original sentence, making it the correct choice.

20. D: A is too general, indicating that an individual will always profit if a company's stock decreases. B indicates that the right to sell shares is contingent on the decrease of a company's stock, which is also not the case. C indicates the individual will profit from a decrease or an increase, but the original sentence clearly states there will be no profit if a stock increases. D tells how an individual can profit if the value of a stock decreases (by purchasing a put), making it the correct choice.

Reading Comprehension

1. B: In describing the marketing of "sea monkeys," the author describes it as creative genius, and attributes their popularity to the drawings and advertisements that appeared in comic books. It is reasonable to conclude that without the branding and (somewhat misleading) ads, they wouldn't have been as popular. Marketing them under the less exciting brand name "brine shrimp" likely wouldn't have resulted in as many sales.

2. C: A is incorrect because the passage states they were similar in size. The cost of production is not mentioned, eliminating B as a possibility. D is incorrect because it was the eight-track tape that was included in these vehicles. C is correct because the passage states the eight-track tape could store and play twice as many songs.

3. B: The passage states that, "Often, the agoraphobic will view his home as the safest possible place to be, and he may even be reluctant to leave his house," making B the correct choice.

4. D: B and C are only briefly mentioned, allowing them to be eliminated as possibilities. Although the passage does discuss what could happen to two balls released at the top of a mountain, that is not the purpose of the passage, so A can be eliminateD.   The purpose is to show how small differences (in this case two inches between two rubber balls) can have large effects. This is essentially what the

- 116 -

butterfly effect is, and the purpose of the passage is to give an example to demonstrate this principle.

5. A: The passage discusses several problems that can occur with wells. Both of the problems mentioned are associated with wells that are too shallow; no problems associated with wells that are too deep are mentioned. Therefore, it seems safe to conclude that a deeper well would be more desirable than a shallow one.

6. C: A is mentioned only briefly in the passage. B and C are mentioned, but this information fits into the overall purpose of the passage, which is to discuss the different types of fats, both good and bad.

7. B: C and D are mentioned only briefly. Although the history of satire is discussed, most of the passage focuses on discussing the three major forms of satire that originated in Ancient Greece and Rome, making B the best choice.

8. A: B is incorrect because the passage states that happiness is expressed similarly by people all over the world. C is incorrect because the passage states that there are many emotions felt and expressed by people all over the world. D is incorrect because, although people may express acceptance differently, that is not sufficient to conclude it is not a natural emotion. A is correct. We can conclude that people can't always hide what they are feeling because of the statement in the passage that the facial expressions associated with emotions like fear are largely involuntary.

9. C: C is the correct answer because the passage mainly focuses on discussing the causes of heat island. A, B, and D are touched upon only in passing.

10. C: A and D are incorrect because the passage states that these are characteristics that marsupials and mammals share. B can be eliminated, because it is not mentioned in the passage. C is the correct choice, as "one thing that separates marsupials from mammals is that their young are born when they are not yet fully-developed" is stated in the passage.

11. B: Theists are the opposite of atheists, so the second sentence provides a contrast to the first.

12. C: The first sentence introduces the concept of home schooling. The second sentence states that one parent usually has to give up their job for home schooling to take place, which is a direct effect of the practice of home schooling.

13. D: The first sentence states that coffee is the most popular beverage. The second sentence directly contradicts it, stating that soda is the most popular. The second sentence contradicts the first.

14. B: A salamander's ability to grow a new tail is an example of the ability to replace severed body parts, which is known as regeneration. The second sentence provides an example of the concept explained in the first.

15. C: Both sentences give the same information, and nothing new is added. The second sentence restates the information from the first.

16. A: The second sentence tells how septic tanks can contribute to the problem of soil contamination. Both contamination and septic tanks are mentioned in the first sentence. Therefore, the second sentence expands on the first.

17. C: The first sentence states that the Richter Scale is the most commonly-used method to measure the strength of earthquakes. The second sentence states that other methods are used more frequently. Therefore, the second sentence contradicts the information in the first.

18. B: The first sentence introduces the concept of adaptation, which refers to an animal's ability to change in order to increase its chances of survival. A porcupine's quills allow it to defend itself against potential predators, thereby increasing its chances of survival. The second sentence provides an example of the concept presented in the first.

19. D: The first sentence states a problem: congestion due to excessive traffic. The second sentence offers a solution: carpooling can reduce the amount of traffic on roads, which could logically help ease congestion.

20. C: The first sentence describes how men make decisions. The second sentence describes the different process that is used by women to make decisions, which provides a contrast to the first.

Arithmetic Test

1. C: When the numerator and denominator of a fraction are divided or multiplied by the same number, the quotient or product is equivalent to the original fraction. In this case, the numerator and denominator of 6/12 can be divided by two, giving 3/6.

2. D: $675 \times 7 = 4{,}725$

3. C: $5{,}465 + 394 = 5{,}859$
This is closest to 6000 (C).

4. C: Multiply 1/6 by 2 to get a common denominator.
$1/6 \times 2 = 2/12$
Then calculate $11/12 - 2/12 = 9/12$
Reduce this fraction by dividing both numerator and denominator by 3.
$(9 \div 3) / (12 \div 3) = 3/4$

- 118 -

5. B: 743 – 87 = 656

6. A: 75 ÷ 16 = 4.6875
Rounded up to the nearest hundredth, the value is 4.69

7. D: 598 × 46 = 27,508

8. B: An easy way to answer this is to convert all of the answer choices to decimals (which can be done by dividing the numerators by the denominators):
1/4 = 0.25
1/3 = 0.33
1/2 = 0.5
3/5 = 0.6
1/3 is the closest to 0.35

9. C: 6.52 + 0.2 + 0.05 = 6.77

10. D: Simply divide the numerator by the denominator to convert the fraction into a decimal.
9 ÷ 5 = 1.8

11. B: 0.058 ÷ 6.37 = 0.009

12. C: Numbers that are fewer places to the right of the decimal point are larger. Since A and B have two zeros and the others have one, they can be eliminated. Since C and D have only one zero, the larger value can be determined by simply looking at the values and ignoring the zeros. 7 is a larger value than 6, so 0.072 represents the largest value.

13. A
First, calculate 12% of 56.
56 × 0.12 = 6.72
Then, add this value (the increase) to the original value of 56.
56 + 6.72 = 62.72
Rounding off, we get 62.7

14. B: We know that the factory produces 12 tonnes of cereal per day. Therefore, to calculate how many days it would take to produce 596 tonnes of cereal, divide 596 by 12.
596 ÷ 12 = 49.67
The factory will need most of the fiftieth day to complete the order.

15. B: One side of a square is 56cm. All of its sides are equal, and the perimeter is the sum of all sides.
Therefore, the perimeter equals 56cm+56cm+56cm+56cm
The perimeter is 224cm.

16. A: There are three fractions: 1/4, 1/8, and 1/2.
To answer the question, they have to be added. The common denominator is 8.
2/8 + 1/8 + 4/8 = 7/8
Among just the first three people, the dog is being taken care of 7/8 of the time.
Now, the time that is left over must be calculated.
Using the common denominator of 8, we know that 1 = 8/8
Therefore, to calculate the proportion of time the fourth person will have to care for the dog:
8/8 – 7/8 = 1/8

17. D: Explanation: First, calculate 3% of 548 meters.
548 meters × 0.03 = 16.44 meters.
Then, add it to the original height.
548 meters + 16.44 meters = 564.44 meters
Rounding off, we get 564 meters.

Elementary Algebra

1. B: 5 × (80 / 8) + (7 – 2) – (9 × 5) =
Remember the order of operations: Parentheses, exponents, multiplication, division, addition, subtraction.
Perform the operations inside the parentheses first:
5 × (10) + (5) – (45) =
Then, do any multiplication and division, working from left to right:
50 + 5 – 45 =
Finally, do any adding or subtracting, working from left to right:
55 – 45 = 10

2. D: – 32 × – 9 + 7 =
When two negatives are multiplied, they become positive:
-32 × -9 = 288
288 + 7 = 295

3. C: 275 – (-64) – 32 =
When a negative number is subtracted from a value, it becomes a positive:
275 – (-64) – 32 =
275 + 64 -32 =
339 – 32 = 307

4. C: $| x \cdot 3 | = 2$
This is an absolute value, indicating $x \cdot 3$ can equal to -2 or 2.
Therefore, we simply have to solve for x in both instances.
$x \cdot 3 = 2$
$x = 2/3$
$x \cdot 3 = -2$

$x = -2/3$

So, $x = -2/3$ or $2/3$

5. A: Since we know the value of x and y, it is simply a matter of substituting them into the expression:

$9x - 3y + 8xy - 3$

$9(10) - 3(-2) + 8(10)(-2) - 3$

$90 + 6 - 160 - 3$

$96 - 163 = -67$

6. B: $9x (3x^2 + 2x - 9)$

To simplify, multiply the value outside of the brackets $(9x)$ by the values inside of the brackets.

$9x \cdot 3x^2 + 9x \cdot 2x - 9x \cdot 9$

$27x^3 + 18 x^2 - 81x$

7. D: $x^5 x^2 + y^0 =$

We know that $x = 3$.

Therefore, we can find the value of $x^5 x^2$

$3^5 3^2$

$243 \cdot 9 = 2,187$

We don't know the value of y, but any value to the power of zero is equal to one. Therefore, $2,187 + 1 = 2,188$

8. A: $(2x - 5)(x+7)$

To expand, multiply the first terms, outside terms, inside terms, and then the last terms (FOIL)

$2x^2 + 14x - 5x - 35$

Combine like terms.

$2x^2 + 9x - 35$

9. C: y represents the number of students who bought a used textbook. Each used textbook cost $50. Therefore, to figure out the total amount spent on used textbooks, the number of students who bought one would have to be multiplied by 50.

Algebraically, this can be represented by $50y$.

10. D: $-4x + 8 \geq 48$

To solve for x, first isolate the variable.

$-4x \geq 48 - 8$

$-4x \geq 40$

Then, divide both sides by -4 to solve for x.

When an inequality is divided by a negative number, the sign must change directions.

$-4x/-4 \geq 40/-4$

- 121 -

$x \leq -10$

11. B: $x^2 + 12x + 36 = 0$
To solve for x, this equation must be factored.
$(x + 6)(x + 6)$
Then, solve for x.
$x + 6 = 0$
$x = -6$

12. A: $56x + 23 = -14$
To solve for x, isolate the variable.
$56x = -14 - 23$
$56x = -37$
$x = -37/56$
To convert to a decimal, divide the numerator by the denominator.
$x = -37 \div 56$
$x = -0.66$

College Level Math Test

1. B: $\underline{64x^4 + 8x^3 - 4x^2 + 16x}$
$ 8x$

To simplify, each term in the numerator can be divided by $8x$ to eliminate the denominator. When variables with an exponent are divided by one another, the exponent in the denominator is subtracted from the exponent in the numerator. When there is no exponent listed, it is assumed to be x^1.
We are left with: $8x^3 + x^2 - 1/2x + 2$

2. C: $9x^2y - 18xy - 27y$
$9y$ is contained in all parts of this expression. Therefore, $9y$ can be factored out.
$9y(x^2 - 2x - 3)$
$(x^2 - 2x - 3)$ can also be factored.
$(x - 3)(x + 1)$
We end up with $9y(x - 3)(x + 1)$

3. A: $\sqrt{3}(5\sqrt{3} - \sqrt{12} + \sqrt{10})$
To simplify, all terms inside the brackets must be multiplied by $\sqrt{3}$
$5\sqrt{3} \times \sqrt{3} - \sqrt{3} \times \sqrt{12} + \sqrt{10} \times \sqrt{3}$
According to the order of operations, multiplication is completed first.
$5\sqrt{9} - \sqrt{36} + \sqrt{30}$
Since the square root of 9 and 36 are whole numbers, this expression can be further simplified.
$5 \times 3 - 6 + \sqrt{30}$
$15 - 6 + \sqrt{30}$
$9 + \sqrt{30}$

4. C: $25x - 12x + 6x - 27 = 35$
To make solving easier, combine like terms.
$19x = 35+27$
$19x = 62$
$x = 62 \div 19$
$x = 3.26$

5. D: $(y + 10)^2 - 625 = 0$
First, move the 625 to the other side of the equation.
$(y + 10)^2 = 625$
Then, take the square root of both sides.
$\sqrt{(y + 10)^2} = \sqrt{625}$
$\sqrt{(y + 10)^2} = \pm25$
$y+10 = 25$ and $y+10 = -25$
Then, it is simply a matter of solving for y
$y + 10 = 25$, so $y = 25 - 10 = 15$
and
$y + 10 = -25$, so $y = -25 - 10 = -35$

6. A: $2x - 6y = 12$
$\quad\quad -6x + 14y = 42$
To solve a variable using a system of equations, one of the variables must be cancelled out. To eliminate x from these equations, first multiply the top equation by 3.
$3(2x - 6y = 12)$
$6x - 18y = 36$
Then, add the two equations to eliminate x.

$\quad 6x - 18y = 36\underline{+ \;\; -6x + 14y = 42}-4y = 78$

Solve for y.
$-4y = 78$
$y = 78/-4$
$y = -19.5$

7. A: Use the first equation to solve for x.
$6x + 2x - 26 = -5x$
$8x + 5x = 26$
$13x = 26$
$x = 2$
Then, evaluate the second equation.
$[(2x - 1)/7]^3$
$[(2 \times 2-1)/7]^3$
$[3/7]^3$
$[0.4285]^3$
$= 0.0787$

- 123 -

Rounding, we get 0.08

8. B: To calculate the slope of a line, we simply have to figure out the change in y over the change in x.

$\dfrac{18 - 2}{-3 - 5}$

$\dfrac{16}{-8} = -2$

-2 is the slope of the line.

9. C: Lines that are perpendicular to each other have inverse slopes.
The slope of the original equation is $-5x$.
The inverse of this is $1/5x$. Both C and D have this slope.
The rest of the equation should remain the same.
The + 27 in choice C is the same as the value in the original equation.
Therefore, choice C is correct.

10. D: To find a midpoint, simply calculate the average of the two sets of points.
For x, the midpoint is calculated in the following manner:
$(-20 + 5)/2 = -7.5$
For y, the midpoint is calculated in the following manner:
$(8 + 3)/2 = 5.5$
The midpoint is $(-7.5, 5.5)$

11. A: To calculate the value of $f(x - 5)$, substitute $(x - 5)$ for x in the given equation.
$f(x) = 4x - 32$
$f(x - 5) = 4(x - 5) - 32$
$f(x - 5) = 4x - 20 - 32$
$f(x - 5) = 4x - 52$

12. B: There are several ways to find the inverse of a function. One way is to switch the y and x in the equation and then solve for x.
$f(x) = 8x + 64$
$y = 8x + 64$
Switch the x and y
$x = 8y + 64$
Then, solve for y.
$-8y = -x + 64$
$y = 1/8x - 8$
This is the value of $f^1(x)$.

13. D: The range of a function is all of the possible values that y can have.
This is a quadratic equation, meaning the graph will be a parabola. The 5 indicates that this is the y intercept of the curve. The slope of the curve is positive, meaning it is sloping upward. Therefore, the lowest value that y can have is five.
So, $y \geq 5$.

14. A: To solve, simply substitute 3 for x.
$f(x) = 9^x 8^x + 6x - 12$
$f(x) = 9^3 \times 8^3 + 6 \times 3 - 12$
$f(x) = 729 \times 512 + 18 - 12$
$f(x) = 373,248 + 6$
$f(x) = 373,254$

15. B: The range of a function is all of the possible values for x. In a standard sine curve, the range is -1 to +1. In the function $y = 3\sin 2x$, there is a vertical stretch of 3. Therefore, the range of this function is all values between -3 and +3.

16. C: To solve this problem, it is necessary to use the Pythagorean Theorem, which states that, in a right triangle, $a^2 + b^2 = c^2$.
Because we are asked to find the length of the hypotenuse, we know that c is the unknown value.
Therefore, $6^2 + 8^2 = c^2$
$36 + 64 = c^2$
$100 = c^2$
To find c, take the square root of both sides.
$\sqrt{100} = \sqrt{c^2}$
$10\text{cm} = c$
17. A
$\dfrac{5}{6i}$
To simplify, multiply the top and bottom by i.
$\dfrac{5 \times i}{6i \times i}$

$\dfrac{5i}{6i^2}$
Using the fact that i^2 is equal to -1, the equation can then be simplified.
$\dfrac{5i}{-6}$
Finally, bring the negative sign out in front.
$-\dfrac{5i}{6}$

18. B: To find the sum of matrices, simply add each value in the first matrix to the value that is in the same position in the second matrix.
In this case, If A = 9 6 5 and B = 5 2 9 the value of A + B is
$\qquad\qquad$ 7 4 6 $\qquad$ 7 4 1
$\qquad\qquad$ 1 1 1 $\qquad$ 8 6 8

9+5 6+2 5+9
7+7 4+4 6+1
1+8 1+6 1+8

- 125 -

= 14 8 14
  14 8   7
   9 7   9

19. C: This is an example of a permutation. We know there are six variables (blocks), so to figure out the number of possible combinations, we must calculate the value of:
$1 \times 2 \times 3 \times 4 \times 5 \times 6 = 720$

20. D: We are given $^{15}P_9$
To express as a factorial, keep the value before the P.
Subtract the value after the P from the first value: $(15 - 9) = 6$
Then, express as a factorial.
$$\frac{15!}{6!}$$

Secret Key #1 - Time is Your Greatest Enemy

Pace Yourself

Wear a watch. At the beginning of the test, check the time (or start a chronometer on your watch to count the minutes), and check the time after each passage or every few questions to make sure you are "on schedule."

If you are forced to speed up, do it efficiently. Usually one or more answer choices can be eliminated without too much difficulty. Above all, don't panic. Don't speed up and just begin guessing at random choices. By pacing yourself, and continually monitoring your progress against your watch, you will always know exactly how far ahead or behind you are with your available time. If you find that you are one minute behind on the test, don't skip one question without spending any time on it, just to catch back up. Take 15 fewer seconds on the next four questions, and after four questions you'll have caught back up. Once you catch back up, you can continue working each problem at your normal pace.

Furthermore, don't dwell on the problems that you were rushed on. If a problem was taking up too much time and you made a hurried guess, it must be difficult. The difficult questions are the ones you are most likely to miss anyway, so it isn't a big loss. It is better to end with more time than you need than to run out of time.

Lastly, sometimes it is beneficial to slow down if you are constantly getting ahead of time. You are always more likely to catch a careless mistake by working more slowly than quickly, and among very high-scoring test takers (those who are likely to have lots of time left over), careless errors affect the score more than mastery of material.

Secret Key #2 - Guessing is not Guesswork

You probably know that guessing is a good idea - unlike other standardized tests, there is no penalty for getting a wrong answer. Even if you have no idea about a question, you still have a 20-25% chance of getting it right.

Most test takers do not understand the impact that proper guessing can have on their score. Unless you score extremely high, guessing will significantly contribute to your final score.

Monkeys Take the Test

What most test takers don't realize is that to insure that 20-25% chance, you have to guess randomly. If you put 20 monkeys in a room to take this test, assuming they answered once per question and behaved themselves, on average they would get 20-25% of the questions correct. Put 20 test takers in the room, and the average will be much lower among guessed questions. Why?

1. The test writers intentionally writes deceptive answer choices that "look" right. A test taker has no idea about a question, so picks the "best looking" answer, which is often wrong. The monkey has no idea what looks good and what doesn't, so will consistently be lucky about 20-25% of the time.

2. Test takers will eliminate answer choices from the guessing pool based on a hunch or intuition. Simple but correct answers often get excluded, leaving a 0% chance of being correct. The monkey has no clue, and often gets lucky with the best choice.

This is why the process of elimination endorsed by most test courses is flawed and detrimental to your performance- test takers don't guess, they make an ignorant stab in the dark that is usually worse than random.

$5 Challenge

Let me introduce one of the most valuable ideas of this course- the $5 challenge:

You only mark your "best guess" if you are willing to bet $5 on it.

You only eliminate choices from guessing if you are willing to bet $5 on it.

Why $5? Five dollars is an amount of money that is small yet not insignificant, and can really add up fast (20 questions could cost you $100). Likewise, each answer choice on one question of the test will have a small impact on your overall score, but it can really add up to a lot of points in the end.

The process of elimination IS valuable. The following shows your chance of guessing it right:

If you eliminate this many choices:	0	1	2	3	4
Chance of getting it correct	20%	25%	33%	50%	100%

However, if you accidentally eliminate the right answer or go on a hunch for an incorrect answer, your chances drop dramatically: to 0%. By guessing among all the answer choices, you are GUARANTEED to have a shot at the right answer.

That's why the $5 test is so valuable- if you give up the advantage and safety of a pure guess, it had better be worth the risk.

What we still haven't covered is how to be sure that whatever guess you make is truly random. Here's the easiest way:

Always pick the first answer choice among those remaining.

Such a technique means that you have decided, **before you see a single test question**, exactly how you are going to guess- and since the order of choices tells you nothing about which one is correct, this guessing technique is perfectly random.

Let's try an example-

A student encounters the following problem on the Mathematics test:

What is $(x^2)(x^3)$ equal to?

    a. x^1
    b. x^5
    c. x^6
    d. x^9

The student has a small idea about this question- he is pretty sure that you are supposed to either add the two exponents (2+3 = 5), or multiply them (2*3 = 6) but he wouldn't bet $5 on either choice. He knows that it isn't any of the other choices and so he is willing to bet $5 on both choices a and d not being correct. So he is down to choices b and c. At this point, he guesses b, since b is the first choice remaining.

The student is correct by choosing b, since $(x^2)(x^3)$ is equal to x^5. He only eliminated those choices he was willing to bet money on, AND he did not let his stale memories (often things not known definitely will get mixed up in the exact opposite arrangement in one's head) about the rules for exponents influence his guess. He blindly chose the first remaining choice, and was rewarded with the fruits of a random guess.

This section is not meant to scare you away from making educated guesses or eliminating choices- you just need to define when a choice is worth eliminating. The

$5 test, along with a pre-defined random guessing strategy, is the best way to make sure you reap all of the benefits of guessing.

Specific Guessing Techniques

Similar Answer Choices

When you have two answer choices that are direct opposites, one of them is usually the correct answer.

Example:

    a. forward

    b. backward

These two answer choices are very similar and fall into the same family of answer choices. A family of answer choices is when two or three answer choices are very similar. Often two will be opposites and one may show an equality.

Example:

    a. excited

    b. overjoyed

    c. thrilled

    d. upset

Note how the first three choices are all related. They all ask describe a state of happiness. However, choice d is not in the same family of questions. Being upset is the direct opposite of happiness.

Summary of Guessing Techniques

1. Eliminate as many choices as you can by using the $5 test. Use the common guessing strategies to help in the elimination process, but only eliminate choices that pass the $5 test.

2. Among the remaining choices, only pick your "best guess" if it passes the $5 test.

3. Otherwise, guess randomly by picking the first remaining choice that was not eliminated.

Secret Key #3 - Practice Smarter, Not Harder

Many test takers delay the test preparation process because they dread the awful amounts of practice time they think necessary to succeed on the test. We have refined an effective method that will take you only a fraction of the time.

There are a number of "obstacles" in your way to succeed. Among these are answering questions, finishing in time, and mastering test-taking strategies. All must be executed on the day of the test at peak performance, or your score will suffer. The test is a mental marathon that has a large impact on your future.

Just like a marathon runner, it is important to work your way up to the full challenge. So first you just worry about questions, and then time, and finally strategy:

Success Strategy

1. Find a good source for practice tests.
2. If you are willing to make a larger time investment, consider using more than one study guide- often the different approaches of multiple authors will help you "get" difficult concepts.
3. Take a practice test with no time constraints, with all study helps "open book." Take your time with questions and focus on applying strategies.
4. Take a practice test with time constraints, with all guides "open book."
5. Take a final practice test with no open material and time limits

If you have time to take more practice tests, just repeat step 5. By gradually exposing yourself to the full rigors of the test environment, you will condition your mind to the stress of test day and maximize your success.

Secret Key #4 - Prepare, Don't Procrastinate

Let me state an obvious fact: if you take the test three times, you will get three different scores. This is due to the way you feel on test day, the level of preparedness you have, and, despite the test writers' claims to the contrary, some tests WILL be easier for you than others.

Since your future depends so much on your score, you should maximize your chances of success. In order to maximize the likelihood of success, you've got to prepare in advance. This means taking practice tests and spending time learning the information and test taking strategies you will need to succeed.

Since you have to pay a registration fee each time you take the test, don't take it as a "practice" test. Feel free to take sample tests on your own, but when you go to take the official test, be prepared, be focused, and do your best the first time!

Secret Key #5 - Test Yourself

Everyone knows that time is money. There is no need to spend too much of your time or too little of your time preparing for the test. You should only spend as much of your precious time preparing as is necessary for you to pass it.

Once you have taken a practice test under real conditions of time constraints, then you will know if you are ready for the test or not.

If you have scored extremely high the first time that you take the practice test, then there is not much point in spending countless hours studying. You are already there.

Benchmark your abilities by retaking practice tests and seeing how much you have improved. Once you score high enough to guarantee success, then you are ready.

If you have scored well below where you need, then knuckle down and begin studying in earnest. Check your improvement regularly through the use of practice tests under real conditions. Above all, don't worry, panic, or give up. The key is perseverance!

Then, when you go to take the test, remain confident and remember how well you did on the practice tests. If you can score high enough on a practice test, then you can do the same on the real thing.

General Strategies

The most important thing you can do is to ignore your fears and jump into the test immediately- do not be overwhelmed by any strange-sounding terms. You have to jump into the test like jumping into a pool- all at once is the easiest way.

Make Predictions

As you read and understand the question, try to guess what the answer will be. Remember that several of the answer choices are wrong, and once you begin reading them, your mind will immediately become cluttered with answer choices designed to throw you off. Your mind is typically the most focused immediately after you have read the question and digested its contents. If you can, try to predict what the correct answer will be. You may be surprised at what you can predict.

Quickly scan the choices and see if your prediction is in the listed answer choices. If it is, then you can be quite confident that you have the right answer. It still won't hurt to check the other answer choices, but most of the time, you've got it!

Answer the Question

It may seem obvious to only pick answer choices that answer the question, but the test writers can create some excellent answer choices that are wrong. Don't pick an answer just because it sounds right, or you believe it to be true. It MUST answer the question. Once you've made your selection, always go back and check it against the question and make sure that you didn't misread the question, and the answer choice does answer the question posed.

Benchmark

After you read the first answer choice, decide if you think it sounds correct or not. If it doesn't, move on to the next answer choice. If it does, mentally mark that answer choice. This doesn't mean that you've definitely selected it as your answer choice, it just means that it's the best you've seen thus far. Go ahead and read the next choice. If the next choice is worse than the one you've already selected, keep going to the next answer choice. If the next choice is better than the choice you've already selected, mentally mark the new answer choice as your best guess.

The first answer choice that you select becomes your standard. Every other answer choice must be benchmarked against that standard. That choice is correct until proven otherwise by another answer choice beating it out. Once you've decided that no other answer choice seems as good, do one final check to ensure that your answer choice answers the question posed.

Valid Information

Don't discount any of the information provided in the question. Every piece of information may be necessary to determine the correct answer. None of the information in the question is there to throw you off (while the answer choices will certainly have information to throw you off). If two seemingly unrelated topics are discussed, don't ignore either. You can be confident there is a relationship, or it wouldn't be included in the question, and you are probably going to have to determine what is that relationship to find the answer.

Avoid "Fact Traps"

Don't get distracted by a choice that is factually true. Your search is for the answer that answers the question. Stay focused and don't fall for an answer that is true but incorrect. Always go back to the question and make sure you're choosing an answer that actually answers the question and is not just a true statement. An answer can be factually correct, but it MUST answer the question asked. Additionally, two answers can both be seemingly correct, so be sure to read all of the answer choices, and make sure that you get the one that BEST answers the question.

Milk the Question

Some of the questions may throw you completely off. They might deal with a subject you have not been exposed to, or one that you haven't reviewed in years. While your lack of knowledge about the subject will be a hindrance, the question itself can give you many clues that will help you find the correct answer. Read the question carefully and look for clues. Watch particularly for adjectives and nouns describing difficult terms or words that you don't recognize. Regardless of if you completely understand a word or not, replacing it with a synonym either provided or one you more familiar with may help you to understand what the questions are asking. Rather than wracking your mind about specific detailed information concerning a difficult term or word, try to use mental substitutes that are easier to understand.

The Trap of Familiarity

Don't just choose a word because you recognize it. On difficult questions, you may not recognize a number of words in the answer choices. The test writers don't put "make-believe" words on the test; so don't think that just because you only recognize all the words in one answer choice means that answer choice must be correct. If you only recognize words in one answer choice, then focus on that one. Is it correct? Try your best to determine if it is correct. If it is, that is great, but if it doesn't, eliminate it. Each word and answer choice you eliminate increases your chances of getting the question correct, even if you then have to guess among the unfamiliar choices.

Eliminate Answers

Eliminate choices as soon as you realize they are wrong. But be careful! Make sure you consider all of the possible answer choices. Just because one appears right, doesn't mean that the next one won't be even better! The test writers will usually put more than one good answer choice for every question, so read all of them. Don't worry if you are stuck between two that seem right. By getting down to just two remaining possible choices, your odds are now 50/50. Rather than wasting too much time, play the odds. You are guessing, but guessing wisely, because you've been able to knock out some of the answer choices that you know are wrong. If you are eliminating choices and realize that the last answer choice you are left with is also obviously wrong, don't panic. Start over and consider each choice again. There may easily be something that you missed the first time and will realize on the second pass.

Tough Questions

If you are stumped on a problem or it appears too hard or too difficult, don't waste time. Move on! Remember though, if you can quickly check for obviously incorrect answer choices, your chances of guessing correctly are greatly improved. Before you completely give up, at least try to knock out a couple of possible answers. Eliminate what you can and then guess at the remaining answer choices before moving on.

Brainstorm

If you get stuck on a difficult question, spend a few seconds quickly brainstorming. Run through the complete list of possible answer choices. Look at each choice and ask yourself, "Could this answer the question satisfactorily?" Go through each answer choice and consider it independently of the other. By systematically going through all possibilities, you may find something that you would otherwise overlook. Remember that when you get stuck, it's important to try to keep moving.

Read Carefully

Understand the problem. Read the question and answer choices carefully. Don't miss the question because you misread the terms. You have plenty of time to read each question thoroughly and make sure you understand what is being asked. Yet a happy medium must be attained, so don't waste too much time. You must read carefully, but efficiently.

Face Value

When in doubt, use common sense. Always accept the situation in the problem at face value. Don't read too much into it. These problems will not require you to make huge leaps of logic. The test writers aren't trying to throw you off with a cheap trick. If you have to go beyond creativity and make a leap of logic in order to have an answer choice answer the question, then you should look at the other answer choices. Don't overcomplicate the problem by creating theoretical relationships or explanations that will warp time or space. These are normal problems rooted in reality. It's just that the applicable relationship or explanation may not be readily apparent and you have to figure things out. Use your common sense to interpret anything that isn't clear.

Prefixes

If you're having trouble with a word in the question or answer choices, try dissecting it. Take advantage of every clue that the word might include. Prefixes and suffixes can be a huge help. Usually they allow you to determine a basic meaning. Pre- means before, post- means after, pro - is positive, de- is negative. From these prefixes and suffixes, you can get an idea of the general meaning of the word and try to put it into context. Beware though of any traps. Just because con is the opposite of pro, doesn't necessarily mean congress is the opposite of progress!

Hedge Phrases

Watch out for critical "hedge" phrases, such as likely, may, can, will often, sometimes, often, almost, mostly, usually, generally, rarely, sometimes. Question writers insert these hedge phrases to cover every possibility. Often an answer choice will be wrong simply because it leaves no room for exception. Avoid answer choices that have definitive words like "exactly," and "always".

Switchback Words

Stay alert for "switchbacks". These are the words and phrases frequently used to alert you to shifts in thought. The most common switchback word is "but". Others include although, however, nevertheless, on the other hand, even though, while, in spite of, despite, regardless of.

New Information

Correct answer choices will rarely have completely new information included. Answer choices typically are straightforward reflections of the material asked about and will directly relate to the question. If a new piece of information is included in an answer choice that doesn't even seem to relate to the topic being asked about, then that answer choice is likely incorrect. All of the information needed to answer the question is usually provided for you, and so you should not have to make guesses that are unsupported or choose answer choices that require unknown information that cannot be reasoned on its own.

Time Management

On technical questions, don't get lost on the technical terms. Don't spend too much time on any one question. If you don't know what a term means, then since you don't have a dictionary, odds are you aren't going to get much further. You should immediately recognize terms as whether or not you know them. If you don't, work with the other clues that you have, the other answer choices and terms provided, but don't waste too much time trying to figure out a difficult term.

Contextual Clues

Look for contextual clues. An answer can be right but not correct. The contextual clues will help you find the answer that is most right and is correct. Understand the context in which a phrase or statement is made. This will help you make important distinctions.

Don't Panic

Panicking will not answer any questions for you. Therefore, it isn't helpful. When you first see the question, if your mind goes blank, take a deep breath. Force yourself to mechanically go through the steps of solving the problem and using the strategies you've learned.

Pace Yourself

Don't get clock fever. It's easy to be overwhelmed when you're looking at a page full of questions, your mind is full of random thoughts and feeling confused, and the clock is ticking down faster than you would like. Calm down and maintain the pace that you have set for yourself. As long as you are on track by monitoring your pace, you are guaranteed to have enough time for yourself. When you get to the last few minutes of the test, it may seem like you won't have enough time left, but if you only have as many questions as you should have left at that point, then you're right on track!

Answer Selection

The best way to pick an answer choice is to eliminate all of those that are wrong, until only one is left and confirm that is the correct answer. Sometimes though, an answer choice may immediately look right. Be careful! Take a second to make sure that the other choices are not equally obvious. Don't make a hasty mistake. There are only two times that you should stop before checking other answers. First is when you are positive that the answer choice you have selected is correct. Second is when time is almost out and you have to make a quick guess!

Check Your Work

Since you will probably not know every term listed and the answer to every question, it is important that you get credit for the ones that you do know. Don't miss any questions through careless mistakes. If at all possible, try to take a second to look back over your answer selection and make sure you've selected the correct answer choice and haven't made a costly careless mistake (such as marking an answer choice that you didn't mean to mark). This quick double check should more than pay for itself in caught mistakes for the time it costs.

Beware of Directly Quoted Answers

Sometimes an answer choice will repeat word for word a portion of the question or reference section. However, beware of such exact duplication – it may be a trap! More than likely, the correct choice will paraphrase or summarize a point, rather than being exactly the same wording.

Slang

Scientific sounding answers are better than slang ones. An answer choice that begins "To compare the outcomes…" is much more likely to be correct than one that begins "Because some people insisted…"

Extreme Statements

Avoid wild answers that throw out highly controversial ideas that are proclaimed as established fact. An answer choice that states the "process should be used in certain situations, if…" is much more likely to be correct than one that states the "process should be discontinued completely." The first is a calm rational statement and doesn't even make a definitive, uncompromising stance, using a hedge word "if" to provide wiggle room, whereas the second choice is a radical idea and far more extreme.

Answer Choice Families

When you have two or more answer choices that are direct opposites or parallels, one of them is usually the correct answer. For instance, if one answer choice states "x increases" and another answer choice states "x decreases" or "y increases," then those two or three answer choices are very similar in construction and fall into the same family of answer choices. A family of answer choices is when two or three answer choices are very similar in construction, and yet often have a directly opposite meaning. Usually the correct answer choice will be in that family of answer choices. The "odd man out" or answer choice that doesn't seem to fit the parallel construction of the other answer choices is more likely to be incorrect.

Sample Question from the Sentence Skills Test

Louisa May Alcott's <u>difficulty over</u> the philosophical brilliance of her father's intellect was tempered by her impatience with his unworldliness

A.   exasperation with

B.   respect for

C.   rebellion against

D.   reverence for

Let's look at a couple of different methods of solving this problem.

1. Understand What to Expect

Before you have read any of the answer choices and begin to stumble over some of the complicated vocabulary words used in the answer choices, see if you can predict what the answer might be, based on the information provided to you in the problem sentence. You aren't trying to guess the exact word that might be in the correct answer choice, but only the type of word that you should expect. Is it a positive word, negative word, etc.

Ask yourself what sort of words would likely fill the blanks provided. Consider that she loved her father and thought highly of him, particularly with regards to his intelligence. Therefore, you should expect a verb with a positive meaning.

Now that you have an idea of what to expect in a correct answer choice, review the choices provided. Choices B and D both have a positive word, "respect" and "reverence" respectively, so either could be correct. Looking further ahead to the second verb in the sentence "tempered," you notice that it means modifying or adjusting. It does make sense that her perception of a positive attribute of her father's would be modified or adjusted by a negative attribute (his unworldliness), making choice D correct.

2. Group the Answers

Review the answer choices and try to identify the common aspects of each answer choice. Are any of the words synonyms or antonyms?

Without ever having looked at the problem, but simply reviewing the answer choices can tell you a lot of information. Classify the words in the answer choice as positive or negative words and group them together. For example, you can tell that both answer choice A and C deal with "anger", using the words "exasperation" and "rebellion". Answer choices B and D deal with "appreciation", using the words "respect" and "reverence".

Grouping answers makes it easy to accept or reject more than one answer at a time. By reviewing the context of the sentence, "appreciation" makes more sense than "anger" in describing a woman's perception of her father's intellectual brilliance. Therefore, answer choices A and C can both be rejected simultaneously, leaving you with choices B and D.

Once again, in comparing the remaining words in choice B and D, "tempered", with its root word "temper" acting as a modifying agent makes choice D the better answer.

3. Make it Easier

As you go through and read the sentence and answer choices, don't allow a complicated wording to confuse you. If you know the meaning of a phrase and it is over complicated, be sure to mentally substitute or scratch through and write above the phrase an easier word that means the same thing.

For example, you can rewrite "Louisa May Alcott's -------- the philosophical brilliance of her father's intellect was tempered by her impatience with his unworldliness" as "Louisa May Alcott's -------- her father's intelligence was tempered by her impatience with his simplicity.

Using words that are simpler and may make it easier for you to understand the true context of the sentence will make it easier for you to identify the correct answer choice. Similarly, you can use synonyms of difficult words as a mental replacement of the words in the answer choices to make it easier for you to understand how the word fits into the sentence.

For example, if you know the meaning of the word "reverence" in choice D, but have difficulty understanding how it fits into the sentence, mentally replace it with the word "appreciation." Appreciation means the same thing and may be easier for you to read and understand in the context of the sentence.

Sample Question from the Arithmetic Test

Three coins are tossed up in the air. What is the probability that two of them will land heads and one will land tails?

A. 0
B. 1/8
C. 1/4
D. 3/8

Let's look at a few different methods and steps to solving this problem.

1. Reduction and Division

Quickly eliminate the probabilities that you immediately know. You know to roll all heads is a 1/8 probability, and to roll all tails is a 1/8 probability. Since there are in total 8/8 probabilities, you can subtract those two out, leaving you with 8/8 – 1/8 – 1/8 = 6/8. So after eliminating the possibilities of getting all heads or all tails, you're left with 6/8 probability. Because there are only three coins, all other combinations are going to involve one of either head or tail, and two of the other. All other combinations will either be 2 heads and 1 tail, or 2 tails and 1 head. Those remaining combinations both have the same chance of occurring, meaning that you can just cut the remaining 6/8 probability in half, leaving you with a 3/8ths chance that there will be 2 heads and 1 tail, and another 3/8ths chance that there will be 2 tails and 1 head, making choice D correct.

2. Run Through the Possibilities for that Outcome

You know that you have to have two heads and one tail for the three coins. There are only so many combinations, so quickly run through them all.

You could have:

H, H, H

H, H, T

H, T, H

T, H, H

T, T, H

T, H, T

H, T, T

T, T, T

Reviewing these choices, you can see that three of the eight have two heads and one tail, making choice D correct.

3. Fill in the Blanks with Symbology and Odds

Many probability problems can be solved by drawing blanks on a piece of scratch paper (or making mental notes) for each object used in the problem, then filling in probabilities and multiplying them out. In this case, since there are three coins being flipped, draw three blanks. In the first blank, put an "H" and over it write "1/2". This represents the case where the first coin is flipped as heads. In that case (where the first coin comes up heads), one of the other two coins must come up tails and one must come up heads to fulfill the criteria posed in the problem (2 heads and 1 tail). In the second blank, put a "1" or "1/1". This is because it doesn't matter what is flipped for the second coin, so long as the first coin is heads. In the third blank, put a "1/2". This is because the third coin must be the exact opposite of whatever is in the second blank. Half the time the third coin will be the same as the second coin, and half the time the third coin will be the opposite, hence the "1/2". Now multiply out the odds. There is a half chance that the first coin will come up "heads", then it doesn't matter for the second coin, then there is a half chance that the third coin will be the opposite of the second coin, which will give the desired result of 2 heads and 1 tail. So, that gives 1/2*1/1*1/2 = 1/4.

But, now you must calculate the probabilities that result if the first coin is flipped tails. So draw another group of three blanks. In the first blank, put a "T" and over it write "1/2". This represents the case where the first coin is flipped as tails. In that case (where the first coin comes up tails), both of the other two coins must come up heads to fulfill the criteria posed in the problem. In the second blank, put an "H" and over it write "1/2". In the third blank, put an "H" and over it write "1/2". Now multiply out the odds. There is a half chance that the first coin will come up "tails", then there is a half chance that the second coin will be heads, and a half chance that the third coin will be heads. So, that gives 1/2*1/2*1/2 = 1/8.

Now, add those two probabilities together. If you flip heads with the first coin, there is a 1/4 chance of ultimately meeting the problem's criteria. If you flip tails with the first coin, there is a 1/8 chance of ultimately meeting the problem's criteria. So, that gives 1/4 + 1/8 = 2/8 + 1/8 = 3/8, which makes choice D correct.

Sample Question from the Reading Comprehension Test

Mark Twain was well aware of his celebrity. He was among the first authors to employ a clipping service to track press coverage of himself, and it was not unusual for him to issue his own press statements if he wanted to influence or "spin" coverage of a particular story. The celebrity Twain achieved during his last ten years still reverberates today. Nearly all of his most popular novels were published before 1890, long before his hair grayed or he began to wear his famous white suit in public. We appreciate the author but seem to remember the celebrity.

Based on the passage above, Mark Twain seemed interested in:

    A. maintaining his celebrity
    B. selling more of his books
    C. hiding his private life
    D. gaining popularity

Let's look at a couple of different methods of solving this problem.

1. Identify the key words in each answer choice. These are the nouns and verbs that are the most important words in the answer choice.

A. maintaining, celebrity
B. selling, books
C. hiding, life
D. gaining, popularity

Now try to match up each of the key words with the passage and see where they fit. You're trying to find synonyms and/or exact replication between the key words in the answer choices and key words in the passage.

A. maintaining – no matches; celebrity – matches in sentences 1, 3, and 5
B. selling – no matches; books – matches with "novels" in sentence 4.
C. hiding – no matches; life – no matches
D. gaining – no matches; popularity –matches with "celebrity" in sentences 1, 3, and 5, because they can be synonyms

At this point there are only two choices that have more than one match, choices A and D, and they both have the same number of matches, and with the same word in the passage, which is the word "celebrity" in the passage. This is a good sign, because the test writers will often write two answer choices that are close. Having two answer choices pointing towards the same key word is a strong indicator that those key words hold the "key" to finding the right answer.

Now let's compare choice A and D and the unmatched key words. Choice A still has "maintaining" which doesn't have a clear match, while choice D has "gaining" which doesn't have a clear match. While neither of those have clear matches in the passage, ask yourself what are the best arguments that would support any kind of connection with either of those two words.

"Maintaining" makes sense when you consider that Twain was interested in tracking his press coverage and that he was actively managing the "spin" of certain stories.

"Gaining" makes sense when you consider that Twain was actively issuing his own press releases, however one key point to remember is that he was only issuing these press releases after another story was already in existence.

Since Twain's press releases were not being released in a news vacuum, but rather as a response mechanism to ensure control over the angle of a story, his releases were more to *maintain* control over his image, rather than *gain* an image in the first place.

Furthermore, when comparing the terms "popularity" and "celebrity", there are similarities between the words, but in referring back to the passage, it is clear that "celebrity" has a stronger connection to the passage, being the exact word used three times in the passage.

Since "celebrity" has a stronger match than "popularity" and "maintaining" makes more sense than "gaining," it is clear that choice A is correct.

2. Use a process of elimination.

A. maintaining his celebrity – The passage discusses how Mark Twain was both aware of his celebrity status and would take steps to ensure that he got the proper coverage in any news story and maintained the image he desired. This is the correct answer.

B. selling more of his books – Mark Twain's novels are mentioned for their popularity and while common sense would dictate that he would be interested in selling more of his books, the passage makes no mention of him doing anything to promote sales.

C. hiding his private life – While the passage demonstrates that Mark Twain was keenly interested in how the public viewed his life, it does not indicate that he cared about hiding his private life, not even mentioning his life outside of the public eye. The passage deals with how he was seen by the public.

D. gaining popularity – At first, this sounds like a good answer choice, because Mark Twain's popularity is mentioned several times. The main difference though is that he wasn't trying to gain popularity, but simply ensuring that the popularity he had was not distorted by bad press.

Sample Topic for the Essay

Possessions can be extremely difficult to give up or lose due to the personal attachment that develops over the years.

Assignment: Do you agree or disagree with the topic statement? Support your position with one or two specific examples from personal experience, the experience of others, current events, history, or literature.

Let's look at a few different methods and steps to solving this problem.

1. What's the Goal?

Remember that on the essay portion of the ACCUPLACER, there isn't a "correct" answer. The response you choose to give to the topic provided does not have to be the first thing that comes to your mind. In fact, the side or response you pick doesn't even have to support the side of the topic that you actually believe in. It is better to have a good explanation for the position, rather than to actually believe in the position on the topic. However, typically you will find that the side you believe in is also the side that you have the most information that you can write about.

To go through some of the steps that you could walk through as you develop your response, let's choose to support the belief that the attachment develops over the years.

As you consider some good examples of possessions, your first thought might be the importance of your home or car, which are necessary for the basic functions of life, such as providing a roof over your head and a method of transportation. Yet, what would be your supporting answer about why your car is important and would be difficult to give up? Some possibilities might be: "it gets me where I need to go, it is brand new, it is expensive, I like it a lot, it would be difficult to replace, it's shiny."

These answer choices may fill up some space, but don't have much meaning. There are other possessions in your life that have much more meaning and priority in other ways that would be better to write about.

Think of possessions that have meaning beyond the mere basics of shelter or transportation. You want a examples that you could potentially write pages and pages about, filling each of them with depths of passionate detail. While you probably won't have time to write pages and pages, it's good to have a examples that have plenty of room to be expanded upon.

2. Make a Short List

The best way to think of examples you would want to include might be to create a short list of possibilities.

What are some that you would truly hate to give up? What are things that you would regret and miss for years to come? What are items that would fit the description of having an emotional attachment develop over the years? Perhaps a precious heirloom, a family antique, or a faded photograph would be suitable examples.

After you've made your list, look back over it and see which possessions you could write the most information about. Those are the ones you would want to include as examples.

3. Answer "Why"

Notice that choosing possessions and writing about them is not the only thing that you have to do. You have to explain your position. You have to answer the "Why."

That is an all-important question. If you wrote a sentence as part of your response and one of the essay scorers looked over your shoulder and said, "but why?" would your next sentence answer their question.

For example, suppose you wrote, "The old chair that used to belong to my grandfather has a lot of meaning."

If someone asked, "But why?" would your next sentence answer it.

Your next sentence should say, "It has meaning because it was the one chair that my grandfather would sit in every day and tell stories from."

Answering the "Why" question is crucial to your success at writing a great essay. It doesn't do any good to write a good essay if it doesn't answer that question.

Sample Question from the College-Level Mathematics Test

Table 1

Length of 0.10 mm diameter aluminum wire(m)	Resistance (ohms) at 20° C
1	3.55
2	7.10
4	14.20
10	35.50

Based on the information in Table 1, one would predict that a 20 m length of aluminum wire with a 0.10 mm diameter would have a resistance of:

A. 16 ohms

B. 25 ohms

C. 34 ohms

D. 71 ohms

Let's look at a few different methods and steps to solving this problem.

1. Create a Proportion or Ratio

The first way you could approach this problem is by setting up a proportion or ratio. You will find that many of the problems on the ACCUPLACER can be solved using this simple technique. Usually whenever you have a given pair of numbers (this number goes with that number) and you are given a third number and asked to find what number would be its match, then you have a problem that can be converted into an easy proportion or ratio.

In this case you can take any of the pairs of numbers from Table 1. As an example, let's choose the second set of numbers (2 m and 7.10 ohms).

Form a question with the information you have at your disposal: 2 meters goes to 7.10 ohms as 20 meters (from the question) goes to which resistance?

From your ratio: 2m/7.10 ohms = 20m/x
"x" is used as the missing number that you will solve for.

Cross multiplication provides us with 2*x = 7.10*20 or 2x = 142.

Dividing both sides by 2 gives us 2x/2 = 142/2 or x = 71, making choice D correct.

2. Use Algebra

The question is asking for the resistance of a 20 m length of wire. The resistance is a function of the length of the wire, so you know that you could probably set up an algebra problem that would have 20 multiplied by some factor "x" that would give you your answer.

So, now you have 20*x = ?

But what exactly is "x"? If 20*x would give you the resistance of a 20 foot piece of wire, than 1*x would give you the resistance of a 1 foot piece of wire. Remember though, the table already told you the resistance of a 1 foot piece of wire – it's 3.55 ohms.

So, if 1*x = 3.55 ohms, then solving for "x" gives you x = 3.55 ohms.

Plugging your solution for "x" back into your initial equation of 20*x = ?, you now have 20*3.55 ohms = 71 ohms, making choice D correct.

3. Look for a Pattern

Much of the time you can get by with just looking for patterns on problems that provide you with a lot of different numbers. In this case, consider the provided table.

1 – 3.55
2 – 7.10
4 – 14.20
10 – 35.50

What patterns do you see in the above number sequences. It appears that when the number in the first column doubled from 1 to 2, the numbers in the second column doubled as well, going from 3.55 to 7.10. Further inspection shows that when the numbers in the first column doubled from 2 to 4, the numbers in the second column doubled again, going from 7.10 to 14.20. Now you've got a pattern, when the first column of numbers doubles, so does the second column.

Since the question asked about a resistance of 20, you should recognize that 20 is the double of 10. Since a length of 10 meant a resistance of 35.50 ohms, then doubling the length of 10 should double the resistance, making 71 ohms, or choice D, correct.

4. Use Logic

A method that works even faster than finding patterns or setting up equations is using simple logic. It appears that as the first number (the length of the wire) gets larger, so does the second number (the resistance).

Since the length of 10 (the largest length wire in the provided table) has a corresponding resistance of 35.50, then another length (such as 20 in the question) should have a length greater than 35.50. As you inspect the answer choices, there is only one answer choice that is greater than 35.50, which is choice D, making it correct.

Special Report: What is Test Anxiety and How Can You Overcome It?

The very nature of tests caters to some level of anxiety, nervousness or tension, just as we feel for any important event that occurs in our lives. A little bit of anxiety or nervousness can be a good thing. It helps us with motivation, and makes achievement just that much sweeter. However, too much anxiety can be a problem; especially if it hinders our ability to function and perform.

"Test anxiety," is the term that refers to the emotional reactions that some test-takers experience when faced with a test or exam. Having a fear of testing and exams is based upon a rational fear, since the test-taker's performance can shape the course of an academic career. Nevertheless, experiencing excessive fear of examinations will only interfere with the test-takers ability to perform, and his/her chances to be successful.

There are a large variety of causes that can contribute to the development and sensation of test anxiety. These include, but are not limited to lack of performance and worrying about issues surrounding the test.

Lack of Preparation

Lack of preparation can be identified by the following behaviors or situations:

Not scheduling enough time to study, and therefore cramming the night before the test or exam

Managing time poorly, to create the sensation that there is not enough time to do everything

Failing to organize the text information in advance, so that the study material consists of the entire text and not simply the pertinent information

Poor overall studying habits

Worrying, on the other hand, can be related to both the test taker, or many other factors around him/her that will be affected by the results of the test. These include worrying about:

Previous performances on similar exams, or exams in general

How friends and other students are achieving

The negative consequences that will result from a poor grade or failure

There are three primary elements to test anxiety. Physical components, which involve the same typical bodily reactions as those to acute anxiety (to be discussed below). Emotional factors have to do with fear or panic. Mental or cognitive issues concerning attention spans and memory abilities.

Physical Signals

There are many different symptoms of test anxiety, and these are not limited to mental and emotional strain. Frequently there are a range of physical signals that will let a test taker know that he/she is suffering from test anxiety. These bodily changes can include the following:

Perspiring

Sweaty palms

Wet, trembling hands

Nausea

Dry mouth

A knot in the stomach

Headache

Faintness

Muscle tension

Aching shoulders, back and neck

Rapid heart beat

Feeling too hot/cold

To recognize the sensation of test anxiety, a test-taker should monitor him/herself for the following sensations:

The physical distress symptoms as listed above

Emotional sensitivity, expressing emotional feelings such as the need to cry or laugh too much, or a sensation of anger or helplessness

A decreased ability to think, causing the test-taker to blank out or have racing thoughts that are hard to organize or control.

Though most students will feel some level of anxiety when faced with a test or exam, the majority can cope with that anxiety and maintain it at a manageable level. However, those who cannot are faced with a very real and very serious condition, which can and should be controlled for the immeasurable benefit of this sufferer.

Naturally, these sensations lead to negative results for the testing experience. The most common effects of test anxiety have to do with nervousness and mental blocking.

Nervousness

Nervousness can appear in several different levels:

The test-taker's difficulty, or even inability to read and understand the questions on the test

The difficulty or inability to organize thoughts to a coherent form

The difficulty or inability to recall key words and concepts relating to the testing questions (especially essays)

The receipt of poor grades on a test, though the test material was well known by the test taker

Conversely, a person may also experience mental blocking, which involves:

Blanking out on test questions

Only remembering the correct answers to the questions when the test has already finished.

Fortunately for test anxiety sufferers, beating these feelings, to a large degree, has to do with proper preparation. When a test taker has a feeling of preparedness, then anxiety will be dramatically lessened.

The first step to resolving anxiety issues is to distinguish which of the two types of anxiety are being suffered. If the anxiety is a direct result of a lack of preparation, this should be considered a normal reaction, and the anxiety level (as opposed to the test results) shouldn't be anything to worry about. However, if, when adequately prepared, the test-taker still panics, blanks out, or seems to overreact, this is not a fully rational reaction. While this can be considered normal too, there are many ways to combat and overcome these effects.

Remember that anxiety cannot be entirely eliminated, however, there are ways to minimize it, to make the anxiety easier to manage. Preparation is one of the best ways to minimize test anxiety. Therefore the following techniques are wise in order to best fight off any anxiety that may want to build.

To begin with, try to avoid cramming before a test, whenever it is possible. By trying to memorize an entire term's worth of information in one day, you'll be shocking your system, and not giving yourself a very good chance to absorb the information. This is an easy path to anxiety, so for those who suffer from test anxiety, cramming should not even be considered an option.

Instead of cramming, work throughout the semester to combine all of the material which is presented throughout the semester, and work on it gradually as the course goes by, making sure to master the main concepts first, leaving minor details for a week or so before the test.

To study for the upcoming exam, be sure to pose questions that may be on the examination, to gauge the ability to answer them by integrating the ideas from your texts, notes and lectures, as well as any supplementary readings.

If it is truly impossible to cover all of the information that was covered in that particular term, concentrate on the most important portions, that can be covered very well. Learn these concepts as best as possible, so that when the test comes, a goal can be made to use these concepts as presentations of your knowledge.

In addition to study habits, changes in attitude are critical to beating a struggle with test anxiety. In fact, an improvement of the perspective over the entire test-taking experience can actually help a test taker to enjoy studying and therefore improve the overall experience. Be certain not to overemphasize the significance of the grade - know that the result of the test is neither a reflection of self worth, nor is it a measure of intelligence; one grade will not predict a person's future success.

To improve an overall testing outlook, the following steps should be tried:

Keeping in mind that the most reasonable expectation for taking a test is to expect to try to demonstrate as much of what you know as you possibly can.

Reminding ourselves that a test is only one test; this is not the only one, and there will be others.

The thought of thinking of oneself in an irrational, all-or-nothing term should be avoided at all costs.

A reward should be designated for after the test, so there's something to look forward to. Whether it be going to a movie, going out to eat, or simply visiting friends, schedule it in advance, and do it no matter what result is expected on the exam.

Test-takers should also keep in mind that the basics are some of the most important things, even beyond anti-anxiety techniques and studying. Never neglect the basic social, emotional and biological needs, in order to try to absorb information. In order to best achieve, these three factors must be held as just as important as the studying itself.

Study Steps

Remember the following important steps for studying:

Maintain healthy nutrition and exercise habits. Continue both your recreational activities and social pass times. These both contribute to your physical and emotional well being.

Be certain to get a good amount of sleep, especially the night before the test, because when you're overtired you are not able to perform to the best of your best ability.

Keep the studying pace to a moderate level by taking breaks when they are needed, and varying the work whenever possible, to keep the mind fresh instead of getting bored.

When enough studying has been done that all the material that can be learned has been learned, and the test taker is prepared for the test, stop studying and do something relaxing such as listening to music, watching a movie, or taking a warm bubble bath.

There are also many other techniques to minimize the uneasiness or apprehension that is experienced along with test anxiety before, during, or even after the examination. In fact, there are a great deal of things that can be done to stop anxiety from interfering with lifestyle and performance. Again, remember that anxiety will not be eliminated entirely, and it shouldn't be. Otherwise that "up" feeling for exams would not exist, and most of us depend on that sensation to perform better than usual. However, this anxiety has to be at a level that is manageable.

Of course, as we have just discussed, being prepared for the exam is half the battle right away. Attending all classes, finding out what knowledge will be expected on the exam, and knowing the exam schedules are easy steps to lowering anxiety. Keeping up with work will remove the need to cram, and efficient study habits will eliminate wasted time. Studying should be done in an ideal location for concentration, so that it is simple to become interested in the material and give it complete attention. A method such as SQ3R (Survey, Question, Read, Recite, Review) is a wonderful key to follow to make sure that the study habits are as effective as possible, especially in the case of learning from a textbook. Flashcards are great techniques for memorization. Learning to take good notes will mean that notes will be full of useful information, so that less sifting will need to be done to seek out what is pertinent for studying. Reviewing notes after class and then again on occasion will keep the information fresh in the mind. From notes that have been taken summary sheets and outlines can be made for simpler reviewing.

A study group can also be a very motivational and helpful place to study, as there will be a sharing of ideas, all of the minds can work together, to make sure that everyone understands, and the studying will be made more interesting because it will be a social occasion.

Basically, though, as long as the test-taker remains organized and self confident, with efficient study habits, less time will need to be spent studying, and higher grades will be achieved.

To become self confident, there are many useful steps. The first of these is "self talk." It has been shown through extensive research, that self-talk for students who suffer from test anxiety, should be well monitored, in order to make sure that it contributes to self confidence as opposed to sinking the student. Frequently the self talk of test-anxious students is negative or self-defeating, thinking that everyone else is smarter and faster, that they always mess up, and that if they don't do well, they'll fail the entire course. It is important to decreasing anxiety that awareness is made of self talk. Try writing any negative self thoughts and then disputing them with a positive statement instead. Begin self-encouragement as though it was a friend speaking. Repeat positive statements to help reprogram the mind to believing in successes instead of failures.

Helpful Techniques

Other extremely helpful techniques include:

Self-visualization of doing well and reaching goals
While aiming for an "A" level of understanding, don't try to "overprotect" by setting your expectations lower. This will only convince the mind to stop studying in order to meet the lower expectations.

Don't make comparisons with the results or habits of other students. These are individual factors, and different things work for different people, causing different results.

Strive to become an expert in learning what works well, and what can be done in order to improve. Consider collecting this data in a journal.

Create rewards for after studying instead of doing things before studying that will only turn into avoidance behaviors.

Make a practice of relaxing - by using methods such as progressive relaxation, self-hypnosis, guided imagery, etc - in order to make relaxation an automatic sensation.

Work on creating a state of relaxed concentration so that concentrating will take on the focus of the mind, so that none will be wasted on worrying.

Take good care of the physical self by eating well and getting enough sleep.

Plan in time for exercise and stick to this plan.

Beyond these techniques, there are other methods to be used before, during and after the test that will help the test-taker perform well in addition to overcoming anxiety.

Before the exam comes the academic preparation. This involves establishing a study schedule and beginning at least one week before the actual date of the test. By doing this, the anxiety of not having enough time to study for the test will be automatically eliminated. Moreover, this will make the studying a much more effective experience, ensuring that the learning will be an easier process. This relieves much undue pressure on the test-taker.

Summary sheets, note cards, and flash cards with the main concepts and examples of these main concepts should be prepared in advance of the actual studying time. A topic should never be eliminated from this process. By omitting a topic because it isn't expected to be on the test is only setting up the test-taker for anxiety should it actually appear on the exam. Utilize the course syllabus for laying out the topics that should be studied. Carefully go over the notes that were made in class, paying special attention to any of the issues that the professor took special care to emphasize while lecturing in class. In the textbooks, use the chapter review, or if possible, the chapter tests, to begin your review.

It may even be possible to ask the instructor what information will be covered on the exam, or what the format of the exam will be (for example, multiple choice, essay, free form, true-false). Additionally, see if it is possible to find out how many questions will be on the test. If a review sheet or sample test has been offered by the professor, make good use of it, above anything else, for the preparation for the test. Another great resource for getting to know the examination is reviewing tests from previous semesters. Use these tests to review, and aim to achieve a 100% score on each of the possible topics. With a few exceptions, the goal that you set for yourself is the highest one that you will reach.

Take all of the questions that were assigned as homework, and rework them to any other possible course material. The more problems reworked, the more skill and confidence will form as a result. When forming the solution to a problem, write out each of the steps. Don't simply do head work. By doing as many steps on paper as possible, much clarification and therefore confidence will be formed. Do this with as many homework problems as possible, before checking the answers. By checking the answer after each problem, a reinforcement will exist, that will not be on the exam. Study situations should be as exam-like as possible, to prime the test-taker's system for the experience. By waiting to check the answers at the end, a psychological advantage will be formed, to decrease the stress factor.

Another fantastic reason for not cramming is the avoidance of confusion in concepts, especially when it comes to mathematics. 8-10 hours of study will become one hundred percent more effective if it is spread out over a week or at least several days, instead of doing it all in one sitting. Recognize that the human brain requires time in order to assimilate new material, so frequent breaks and a span of study time over several days will be much more beneficial.

Additionally, don't study right up until the point of the exam. Studying should stop a minimum of one hour before the exam begins. This allows the brain to rest and put things in their proper order. This will also provide the time to become as relaxed as possible when going into the examination room. The test-taker will also have time to eat well and eat sensibly. Know that the brain needs food as much as the rest of the body. With enough food and enough sleep, as well as a relaxed attitude, the body and the mind are primed for success.

Avoid any anxious classmates who are talking about the exam. These students only spread anxiety, and are not worth sharing the anxious sentimentalities.

Before the test also involves creating a positive attitude, so mental preparation should also be a point of concentration. There are many keys to creating a positive attitude. Should fears become rushing in, make a visualization of taking the exam, doing well, and seeing an A written on the paper. Write out a list of affirmations that will bring a feeling of confidence, such as "I am doing well in my English class," "I studied well and know my material," "I enjoy this class." Even if the affirmations aren't believed at first, it sends a positive message to the subconscious which will result in an alteration of the overall belief system, which is the system that creates reality.

If a sensation of panic begins, work with the fear and imagine the very worst! Work through the entire scenario of not passing the test, failing the entire course, and dropping out of school, followed by not getting a job, and pushing a shopping cart through the dark alley where you'll live. This will place things into perspective! Then, practice deep breathing and create a visualization of the opposite situation - achieving an "A" on the exam, passing the entire course, receiving the degree at a graduation ceremony.

On the day of the test, there are many things to be done to ensure the best results, as well as the most calm outlook. The following stages are suggested in order to maximize test-taking potential:

Begin the examination day with a moderate breakfast, and avoid any coffee or beverages with caffeine if the test taker is prone to jitters. Even people who are used to managing caffeine can feel jittery or light-headed when it is taken on a test day.

Attempt to do something that is relaxing before the examination begins. As last minute cramming clouds the mastering of overall concepts, it is better to use this time to create a calming outlook.

Be certain to arrive at the test location well in advance, in order to provide time to select a location that is away from doors, windows and other distractions, as well as giving enough time to relax before the test begins.

Keep away from anxiety generating classmates who will upset the sensation of stability and relaxation that is being attempted before the exam.

Should the waiting period before the exam begins cause anxiety, create a self-distraction by reading a light magazine or something else that is relaxing and simple.

During the exam itself, read the entire exam from beginning to end, and find out how much time should be allotted to each individual problem. Once writing the exam, should more time be taken for a problem, it should be abandoned, in order to begin another problem. If there is time at the end, the unfinished problem can always be returned to and completed.

Read the instructions very carefully - twice - so that unpleasant surprises won't follow during or after the exam has ended.

When writing the exam, pretend that the situation is actually simply the completion of homework within a library, or at home. This will assist in forming a relaxed atmosphere, and will allow the brain extra focus for the complex thinking function.

Begin the exam with all of the questions with which the most confidence is felt. This will build the confidence level regarding the entire exam and will begin a quality momentum. This will also create encouragement for trying the problems where uncertainty resides.

Going with the "gut instinct" is always the way to go when solving a problem. Second guessing should be avoided at all costs. Have confidence in the ability to do well.

For essay questions, create an outline in advance that will keep the mind organized and make certain that all of the points are remembered. For multiple choice, read every answer, even if the correct one has been spotted - a better one may exist.

Continue at a pace that is reasonable and not rushed, in order to be able to work carefully. Provide enough time to go over the answers at the end, to check for small errors that can be corrected.

Should a feeling of panic begin, breathe deeply, and think of the feeling of the body releasing sand through its pores. Visualize a calm, peaceful place, and include all of the sights, sounds and sensations of this image. Continue the deep breathing, and take a few minutes to continue this with closed eyes. When all is well again, return to the test.

If a "blanking" occurs for a certain question, skip it and move on to the next question. There will be time to return to the other question later. Get everything done that can be done, first, to guarantee all the grades that can be compiled, and to build all of the confidence possible. Then return to the weaker questions to build the marks from there.

Remember, one's own reality can be created, so as long as the belief is there, success will follow. And remember: anxiety can happen later, right now, there's an exam to be written!

After the examination is complete, whether there is a feeling for a good grade or a bad grade, don't dwell on the exam, and be certain to follow through on the reward that was promised...and enjoy it! Don't dwell on any mistakes that have been made, as there is nothing that can be done at this point anyway.

Additionally, don't begin to study for the next test right away. Do something relaxing for a while, and let the mind relax and prepare itself to begin absorbing information again.

From the results of the exam - both the grade and the entire experience, be certain to learn from what has gone on. Perfect studying habits and work some more on confidence in order to make the next examination experience even better than the last one.

Learn to avoid places where openings occurred for laziness, procrastination and day dreaming.

Use the time between this exam and the next one to better learn to relax, even learning to relax on cue, so that any anxiety can be controlled during the next exam. Learn how to relax the body. Slouch in your chair if that helps. Tighten and then relax all of the different muscle groups, one group at a time, beginning with the feet and then working all the way up to the neck and face. This will ultimately relax the muscles more than they were to begin with. Learn how to breathe deeply and comfortably, and focus on this breathing going in and out as a relaxing thought. With every exhale, repeat the word "relax."

As common as test anxiety is, it is very possible to overcome it. Make yourself one of the test-takers who overcome this frustrating hindrance.

Appendix: Area, Volume, Surface Area Formulas

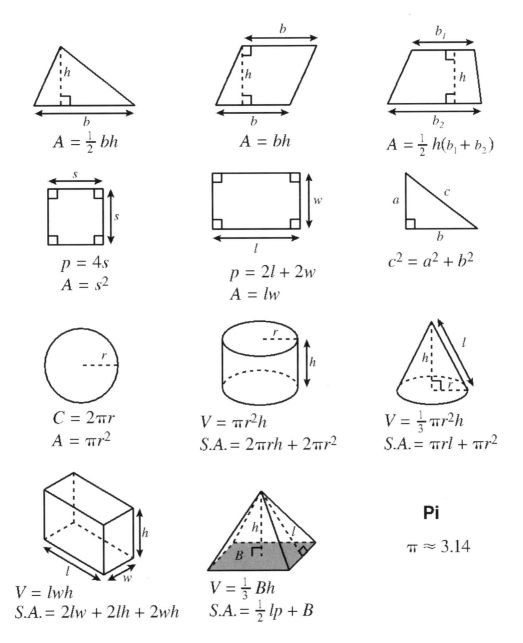

$A = \frac{1}{2}bh$

$A = bh$

$A = \frac{1}{2}h(b_1 + b_2)$

$p = 4s$
$A = s^2$

$p = 2l + 2w$
$A = lw$

$c^2 = a^2 + b^2$

$C = 2\pi r$
$A = \pi r^2$

$V = \pi r^2 h$
$S.A. = 2\pi rh + 2\pi r^2$

$V = \frac{1}{3}\pi r^2 h$
$S.A. = \pi rl + \pi r^2$

$V = lwh$
$S.A. = 2lw + 2lh + 2wh$

$V = \frac{1}{3}Bh$
$S.A. = \frac{1}{2}lp + B$

Pi

$\pi \approx 3.14$

Special Report: Additional Bonus Material

Due to our efforts to try to keep this book to a manageable length, we've created a link that will give you access to all of your additional bonus material.

Please visit http://www.mometrix.com/bonus948/accuplacer to access the information.